THE CALL OF THE
WILDERNESS

A TRAPPER'S TALE

Dave Vander Meer

iUniverse LLC
Bloomington

THE CALL OF THE WILDERNESS
A TRAPPER'S TALE

iUniverse books may be ordered through booksellers or by contacting:

iUniverse
1663 Liberty Drive
Bloomington, IN 47403
www.iuniverse.com
1-800-Authors (1-800-288-4677)

ISBN: 978-1-4917-2973-1 (sc)
ISBN: 978-1-4917-2975-5 (hc)
ISBN: 978-1-4917-2974-8 (e)

Library of Congress Control Number: 2014905314

Printed in the United States of America.

iUniverse rev. date: 03/20/2014

CONTENTS

INTRODUCTON

Walk the trails, and paddle the wilderness lakes, as you travel along on a wilderness, trapline adventure. Experience the thrill of a first catch, and the adrenaline rush as you match wits with wolves, weather and the ever finicky Mother Nature. From an attempted moose rescue, to a near death moment, to being surrounded by a pack of wolves, you will feel what it was like to be dropped into the middle of the northern Ontario wilderness, dozens of miles from the nearest person. No shelter but what you can make for yourself, and only your wits and your trusty dog to keep you alive.

In writing this book I have, after the umpteenth time finally responded to all the folks whom, after hearing about some of the things that had happened to me over the many years, while trapping in the northern wilderness, said "Oh my lord, you should write a book or something." As most that have lived this kind of life will attest, our adventures are mostly looked upon as every day happenings, and sometimes we forget that too many it may be an interesting story. Reading back over my journals over the years led me to want to share these experiences with others, to enjoy, as I have enjoyed reading every trapping related book that is available.

But mostly this book was written for my children, and my two beautiful granddaughters, Alexis and Mackayla, so they can read about PAPA's adventures back in the day; in the real world, when things only now seem to happen in a virtual world. To all others, I hope you enjoy this read as much as I have enjoyed writing it. It truly brought me back to the point that I was living it all over again, and suddenly I realized that yes, the things that happened back then maybe were exciting, and dangerous, but they didn't seem all that special at the time. This is an account, to let the reader know what it felt like to be there, with a day by day, and at times an hour by hour telling of my first two month solo adventure into the wilderness that was to become such a major part of my life.

GOOD-BYE TO CIVILIZATION

(November 1, 1978)

I turned from the mountain of supplies as the engine of the Beaver float plane roared over the sound of the wind and the waves. I watched as the plane picked up speed, the prop turning spray into mist as it bounced across the top of the waves on Hiawatha Lake, my new home, on its way back to Hearst in northern Ontario.

The pilot cleared water and slowly lifted the aircraft over the trees. Banking gently above my new cabin site, he dipped his wings to me, and I waved a good-bye and thanks to my last connection to civilization. Watching as the plane slowly disappeared into the north eastern horizon, the sound of his engine having long ago been carried away by the wind, I turned back to the huge task at hand; the job of moving a mountain of supplies from their present position on the lake shore to the top of the hill where I planned on building my cabin. Supplies that were to last the almost two months I would be here before the planes return on December 23 rd.

Glancing down at Lobo, my Husky/Samoyed cross companion, I realized that he was not going to be much help. "Better get it in gear then Dave," I told myself, and with that I grabbed a load from the pile that contained everything I owned and headed up the hill. Trip after trip, up the hill down the hill and back again. About the third trip or so, a shadow moved across the ground. A couple of Canada jays or Whiskey jacks had come for a visit. "Well that didn't take you long did it," I mumbled to them. "Already looking for a hand out are you?"

But the birds were nice to have around, and as I travelled up and down they kept pace until they finally figured that the chance of getting free food from me right now was nil. Off they went to parts unknown, and I kept up the hurried pace until all my gear was moved. Traps, food, equipment, axes, sleeping bag, snowshoes, tent, woodstove, lantern and the myriad of other items needed to stay in the bush and harvest the furbearers that I was sure were just out of my eyesight, watching and trying to figure out what I was doing there.

Step one was to set up the tent, my temporary home until I had a cabin built. Being just a six by ten nylon tent with a fly it was only about fifteen minutes before the tent was able to start protecting my food from the weather and the critters. With my traps piled in one area, my building material and tools stacked where I was thinking of building the cabin and with my spare clothes and sleeping bag inside with the food, my stomach finally told me it was time for lunch.

Down at the lake shore there were some nice rocks to build a fire pit. Sure a few more trips up and down that hill wouldn't bother me. But then I got smart! Taking my big woods # 1 canvas packsack I loaded it with good sized rocks and only needed two trips to get all I needed. Grabbing a few dead branches from the bottom of a nearby jack pine I broke them up and peeling a little birch bark off a tree there was a nice fire going in no time.

Cracking a can of beef stew I set it beside the flames and went to get a five gallon pail of water from the lake. Soon with my stew all heated up, the water at a rolling boil and a plan of action in my head, I filled my belly, enjoyed my very first wilderness coffee and got right to work.

All I really wanted to do though was go out and set some traps. The trapping season for water animals (beaver, muskrat, otter and mink) had actually opened up two weeks ago and the dry fur (marten, fox, wolves, fisher and lynx) had opened one week previous. Since my scheduled arrival had been delayed by two weeks I really should have had a cabin built by now and most of my traps out. With today being November the 1st, I was under the gun to get things moving quickly.

As important as the cabin was a good wood supply, and thankfully that was not going to be an issue because the lake was lined with dead trees just a short carry from where I was standing. Coming from southern Ontario I had no idea when and how hard winter would hit but I needed to be ready for it, and I was sure it was not that far off. I remembered hearing from someone that anytime after the 7th of November you could expect the lakes to freeze, and that did not give me much time. No use worrying about it though, because it was what it was!

Picking out a nice cabin site, I next went to locate some good straight trees to cut down for the cabin walls. With no actual lumber of any sort other than my beaver stretchers (and they were needed elsewhere) I was planning on a dirt floor and maybe seven foot walls. I figured a 16 X 12 foot floor space would be plenty big enough, so I cut a couple of trees and measured off an 18 and a 14 foot piece from each tree. The tops I limbed and set aside for roof poles. For the walls I used nothing smaller than 6 inches at the narrow end.

Four wall poles were now cut so I decided to move them to the building site. Standing the first one on its end I slid my shoulder to the middle and let the log slowly tip till it is rested on my shoulder. Holy crap that thing was heavy! I stiff legged it to the cabin site and dropped it on the ground thinking that the log probably weighed twice as much as I did. No, I thought to myself that was not going to work. With an average thickness of maybe 8 inches and 7 foot walls I was going to need 40 to 50 logs.

Taking a quick walk around the site, I realized that there were not near that many good straight trees within a close enough distance to make this possible. And to carry them all would probably break my shoulder. Time to rethink this deal! Maybe going and setting a few traps before dark would help me think it through. Funny how you can rationalize anything when you want it bad enough hey! And right now, what I wanted was to set some traps. Throwing a couple #330 conibears, the big square beaver traps, a few smaller #120 conibears and some foothold traps into my pack along with wire, pliers, an axe and grabbing my model 9422 Winchester lever action 22, I was ready.

While in the plane, with the pilot circling the water, I had noticed a beaver lodge on the south end of the lake, just inside the river where it exited toward Nagagami Lake. That was where I would head first, I decided, as I walked down the hill toward my canoe.

Tossing everything inside the watercraft, I remembered my fishing gear and headed back up the hill to retrieve it. I called the dog and in he got, curled up on the floor and I stepped in. Sitting down on the front seat, but facing the back of the canoe, I pushed off. There was still a medium strength wind blowing from the north, so I headed straight across the lake to the point a half mile away. The waves lapped at the side of the canoe and I got some splash on me but nothing serious. At the point I noted to myself that this would be a perfect mink set location but first I needed some bait.

With that revelation echoing in my head I set my fishing rod up and within minutes I was on the move. A three and a half inch red devil trailing behind attached to my 15 lb test line. Now, being behind the point, the wind had no real affect on me. Moving at a good trolling speed, a strong j-stroke pushing us through the blue waters with an ease that comes from much practice, I couldn't believe that I was actually there. The feeling of paddling across a wilderness lake, for the first time, knowing that for the next two months you will have no contact with the rest of the world, well… It is an amazing feeling, like you are the only person on earth. Yes, I was finally home!

By the time I arrived at the beaver house I had a nice three pound northern pike in the boat. Supper was looking real good now! There was a perfect entrance at the house in about two feet of water and it took me only a few minutes to make the set. Throwing in a slide set, where the beavers had been pushing mud up onto the house for the winter's insulation, I also added a rock cubby mink set behind the lodge. Using a #1 foot trap with a drown wire, I chopped the head off the fish and placed it in the back of the cubby. With the trap in an inch of water, I placed dry grass all around the set and it was open for business. I had figured out already that if you are going to stop to set a beaver trap, you may as well have a mink, muskrat and or a marten set there as well. So much time is spent travelling and stopping that you need to make productive use of the time you spend not moving.

Back in the canoe, I pointed the bow west and with the wind having died a little, I took the west shore back to camp. A half an hour and two Northerns later I beached the canoe at my docking site as Lobo bailed out. I followed closely, dragging my gear along with the fish as I headed up the hill. With the coffee pot still hot over the coals I mixed up a cup and sat down to build a marten box. These boxes which I had not pre-constructed, to save on space in the plane, were made of four pieces of 1 x 8 x ¾ inch lumber cut into 16 inch lengths. Nailing them into a square they formed a sort of hollow log that had a 6 and3/4 inch hole, which was the perfect size for a # 120 conibear trap. With 2 notches cut in opposite sides of the top for the trap springs to fit in, a ½ inch hole drilled into one of the opposite boards and the bottom covered with 3 to the inch hardware cloth (which is a heavy wire screen) the box was ready for use.

It could be used hanging in a tree for marten, on a dead log or on the lake shore for mink. This particular box was going into a tree behind the campsite right now. Grabbing my axe, a trap, some wire, and the box with a fish head in it I moved about 100 yards back from the camp site, and in a nice big white spruce tree I hammered a 5 inch nail into the tree about 6 feet from the ground. Leaving the nail sticking out about 1 and ½ inches I slid the box onto it, set the trap in the entrance and wired the trap chain to a sturdy branch, so that when caught the animal would hang 4 to 5 feet of the ground.

This entire set took maybe 10 minutes to put in and on the way back I chopped down a nice dry jack pine tree for the woodpile. Pulling it back with me, I bucked it up with my saw and after splitting the biggest pieces, piled it beside my fire pit. With the sun setting behind me as I cooked supper, I couldn't believe that I had landed here a scant 10 hours earlier. A delicious meal of fish and fried potatoes over an open fire is like nothing you can get in any restaurant in the world. With the rest of my fish stored away in a pot I fed Lobo some dry dog food and set to building the rest of my marten boxes.

Working by firelight, I had after a few hours, the rest of them put together and stacked between two trees. Finally with my bedroll laid out and Lobo sleeping outside the door, I crawled into bed and relaxed. I just laid there listening to the quiet... and some splashing in the lake. Who knows, a late flight of ducks on their way south, or maybe a moose walking along the shore. Whatever it was, Lobo growled a light warning as I drifted off to sleep contemplating what had brought me to this place in time.

THE BEGINNING

(October, 1969)

At 10 years of age I was an avid reader and often found in the school library. A book beckoned me! Traplines North. I picked it up, opened the front cover and for the next four years the book was never out of my mind or far from my hands. The story of a young man, 18 year old Jim Vander beck, who due to his father's illness was left along with his brother Lindsay Jr. to tend the families traplines. This book along with others like Mink, Mary and Me by Chick Ferguson, North to Cree Lake by Alex Karrass and many others stirred in me a need to see these wild places. The thought of standing somewhere that had never seen a human foot print was an amazing feeling.

When and why this love of the bush developed in me is still a mystery. My dad would take us fishing and camping several times a year, but never did anyone in my family go hunting or trapping. One spring day, at the age of 13, I was fishing the North River, just a few miles from my home town of Orillia, Ontario. I had biked there from school and while walking along the shore, I noticed a trap set under an upturned root on the river bank. Regretting it to this day I took the trap and reset it downstream a ways. (I only mention it now because the statute of limitations has run out). The next day I could not wait for school to end. The bell rang and I flew out the doors. At the river I hurried downstream to the trap and low and behold there was my first muskrat.

Trapping has been a huge part and a driving force in my life since that day, from that moment forward every penny I could scrape together was saved to buy traps. To me it was like a high interest savings plan. Save 5 dollars, invest it in a trap and over the year get a return of several hundred percent. Worked for me! I ran paper routes, collected pop and beer bottles, cut lawns, shoveled driveways and generally did anything that would make me a buck.

At 14 my dad figured he should get a trapping license so I could actually start selling furs. Being a very small kid, I would have to get my dad to set the # 330 conibears for me at home. With a safety on them I would ride my bike to my trapping spot and make the set. If I caught something, I would load it in my pack and bring it home for him to remove. Then start all over again.

There was an age limit of 16 to get a license so for two years the furs were sold under his name. At 16 I got my hunting and trapping license and at dinner with my family (three brothers and two sisters) one night my dad asked if I would be interested in taking a trapping course. I leaped at the opportunity! The course was being held at Georgian College in Barrie and was being put on by Lloyd Cook. I did not know it at the time but Lloyd would turn out to be, over the next two years, one of the most influential people in my life. The long time president of the Ontario Trappers Association, Lloyd was a staunch promoter of humane trapping and wildlife conservation.

With his pet beaver "Thumper" Lloyd would put on clinics and courses, teaching new trappers and old alike. Watching this thin, small (in stature only) man stick his hand in a # 4 double long spring to dispel the myth of the trap crushing bones on impact was impressive to say the least. Maybe at the time I thought a little crazy also. But he was truly an inspiration to me and I enjoyed every minute I was able to spend with him.

At the course Lloyd had mentioned that there was a convention in North Bay, Ontario near the end of February. Now North Bay was

130 miles from my home and when I asked my parents if I could go they were not very cooperative and said there was no way I was missing two days of school. So Thursday morning when my dad dropped my brother and myself off at the school I walked in one door and out the back, climbed the fence, slid down the hill and was on the shoulder of HWY # 11. A straight shot from there to North Bay!

Sticking my thumb out it took no time to get a ride. Being a small guy of about 120 pounds at that age, I think a lot of people felt sorry for me because I have never had trouble hitching rides. My first ride took me to Bracebridge and from there one more ride and I was on the streets of North Bay. Now what to do? I had no idea where this convention was taking place, or even how much a hotel room cost but I knew I was finding the cheapest room in North Bay to stay in. That was so like me, don't think about it... just go do it!

Finding a room, I inquired at the front desk as to where the OTA convention was being held. The other end of town of course so calling a cab I headed that way. Walking through the front doors I was awe struck! Here was an entire huge building, full of anything that I might want to know about the only thing I wanted to do with my life. I was truly in heaven! The next three days were a blur as I mingled around, listening to the grizzled old trappers telling each other tales of trapping ,hunting and general bush talk. I tried to blend in and just watch, absorbing all the info I could.

At one point on Friday night Lloyd walked by. I had seen him moving around the convention but did not want to bother him. This time however he noticed me. "Dave" he said. "Glad you made it. Convinced your dad did you." "Well sorta "I replied. "Come with me" he said, and with that he introduced me to some of the legends of trapping in Ontario. Guys like Mangus Nyman the marten king from Chapleau, and Paul Mallette' from Hearst, who was catching hundreds of beaver a year. It all amazed me to the point that I was able to forget the trouble I would be in upon my return home.

After what was the most incredible weekend of my life to that point it was time to go home. Having not spent all of my money and the fact that it was dark out by the time the festivities were finished I decided to catch a bus home instead of hitching in the dark.

When I walked through the door of my house, well let's just say that there had been a slight upheaval in the force while I was gone. On top of me going, after being told not to, the school had called on Friday and informed my parents that I had not been there in over a month. Well thanks a lot there school… my dad flipped! But I was adamant, I was not going back and no amount of arguing would change my mind. I did not need an education to go trapping. Give me a break… I was 16… what did I know.

My dad said that if I didn't want to go to school then I was getting a job, I was not bumming around all day. I think he figured that by getting me a job doing dishes that would entice me back into school. Are you kidding! Now I had money to buy all kinds of traps. Sorry dad, nice try though.

That spring I got a job at a fishing resort and all my money was spent on trapping supplies. The owners gave me a canoe at the end of the summer as a bonus. Awesome!!! When I got back to Orillia I found out I was the proud owner of a 1967 International Travelall. A huge 4 wheel drive suburban type vehicle. My dads car had fried so he had taken my spring trapping check that totaled $1800.00 and used it to buy this truck. I loved it!

Trapping that year was great. I could venture farther and was finally able to set the big traps myself now. Beaver, coons, rats, mink and fox were all on my menu. I even picked up a coyote in a fox snare one day. It was wonderful but in the back of my mind those books still haunted me.

The next summer I went to work again at the fishing lodge but things did not work out and soon made my way back home. I had left the vehicle for my dad to use for work, and so I decided that I was going to look for a real trap line up north. Loading my pack with some food, a tarp, sleeping bag and some cooking utensils I was off. Hitchhiking my way north I stopped at any conservation office I could find.

I would fill out an application for a trap line and move on. The whole summer found me traveling from town to town. North Bay, New Liskeard, Cochrane, Timmins, Gogama, Kapuskasing, Hearst and on until I saw the sign, Nakina! The home of the book, "Traplines North" that had started this adventure. The town was quite away off the main highway and after a couple days of little traffic I gave up and put a request in at Geraldton, the closest town to Nakina. I would spend a few days fishing here and there and if I saw a nice river I would ask to be dropped off. Fish for a day and get back on the road.

After a month or so I was back in Orillia waiting for trapping season. While there, the town officials contacted me and asked if I would trap a beaver house that was within city limits and the beavers were cutting down trees on some local properties. "Sure" I told them, "but not till the season was open in two weeks." That was fine with them, so I set up the house and in the course of a week took 17 beavers out of one house, by far the most I had ever seen come from one colony.

That spring found me on the road again, hitching rides across Ontario looking for a place to trap. Spending a lot of time in White River on HWY # 17, I got a job working at the Green Gables Hotel as a bar tender. I had just turned 18 in July and working every day I met a lot of guys that trapped in the area. In September my Dad called and told me there was a letter from the ministry office in Gogama. Thanking Dennie Morin for the job I caught a bus back to Orillia to see what the letter was all about. By the time I got there another letter had come from the Hearst office. Both letters were offering me a trap line in their areas.

With each letter was a map of the lines that were available to me. Each letter stated plainly that the lines were very remote and that there were inherent dangers involved with accepting a line in these areas. In hindsight maybe my mom should not have been allowed to read that part, but I think they knew there was no stopping this now.

The Hearst line was the most remote, so of course I chose that one. It also happened to be only an hour and a half from White River. Now the planning started in earnest. I informed the Hearst office that I was accepting the trap line that was mentioned in the letter, and I would be there by the middle of October to get my license and head into the bush.

Next came the packing, all my trapping equipment, camping gear, hunting and fishing equipment and the million little things I might need. With the plan being to fly in on October the 15th, I phoned the ministry office in Hearst and asked if they knew the name of the floatplane base in the area. With the number in hand I called and made a reservation. Buying as much food as my money would allow, I loaded it all into the truck, whistled for the dog and waved goodbye to what had been my home for my whole life.

Arriving in White River late that night, after a long twelve hour drive, I realized that I needed more money to buy lumber for marten boxes and more food. What I had left was only enough for the airplane ride into Hiawatha Lake. Just the name itself sounded romantic. Dennie was nice enough to let me work for a couple weeks to get enough funds to purchase what was needed.

Finally on October the 31st, I was set. I headed north, me and my dog on the adventure of a life time. But once again fate stepped in to delay me. Travelling east on HWY # 11, a van coming toward me suddenly swerved and the wheels hit the gravel, sending the vehicle into a flying rollover. It landed on its wheels in the ditch, bounced once and flipped again. This time it landed in the middle of a small river. Pulling off the road and into the ditch beside the river, I jumped out and there floating in the river was, "Oh no, not a baby". I jumped in up to my waist and grabbed the infant as the mother crawled, screaming, through the gaping hole where the windshield had been.

Handing her the child, I dragged her from the water and drove down to a gas station about a mile away. Stopping to phone for an ambulance, the lady was transferred to a faster vehicle than my old truck and they took off to meet the paramedics. For the rest of the day I was giving statements and waiting while the police did their thing.

While I was waiting a truck pulled up and out pops who, but Paul Mallette'. I was standing in the middle of his trap line! In the back of his truck was his mornings catch. 28 beavers! What the… that's almost as much as I caught all last year. And it was only 2 o'clock in the pm. What a trapper! We chatted for awhile, with Paul quizzing me on what I was doing here. "Just be careful" he told me, "there are a lot of things out there in the bush that can ruin your day in a hurry." Finally I was allowed to leave, but by that time the ministry office was closed and I would have to wait till the next day to start the rest of my life.

I spent the night in my vehicle watching ghosts and goblins prowling the streets. Yes I know, but it was the 31st remember. Halloween!

Bright and early the next morning I was at the game wardens office at 8 o'clock sharp, having already had a good breakfast. I paid for my license and the game warden handed me a map, stating that if I needed to, the train tracks were straight south about 23 miles from Hiawatha Lake. Once there I could flag down a train and catch a ride into Hornepayne. Oh… ok… just 23 miles! No problem I'll get right on it. After the regular questions like "Are you sure you know what you are doing", and "have you ever done this sort of thing before" all of which had no bearing on my decision, I headed out. I was doing what I was born to do.

Finally moving again I headed back west for ten miles or so to the floatplane base. I was a little worried since I could see no planes in the water. Just the ones pulled up on shore. Then I noticed a guy walking from a hanger and he asked if I was Dave. Looking at all the gear I had he laughed, "Are you going to try and get all that into one plane". "Well" I replied "I do kind of need everything". "If the pilot will load it all I guess it will be o.k. then". He said my plane would be back shortly, and I could start unloading on the dock. Even before the gear was all emptied from my vehicle the sound of an incoming plane reached my ears. Watching, he came in just over the tree line and settled easily into the water. Moments later he was tied up to the dock and digging for straps to hold down the canoe.

And then the loading began. Now this guy had loaded planes before. I would hand him something and he would say "Not that, something smaller" or "something bigger". Looking at the inside of the plane and back at my pile I was sure there was no way it was all going in there. But like the pro that he was, he made it all fit. Even had a tiny spot on top of it all, for Lobo to sit on. Finally with the canoe strapped onto the float struts we were ready to go. The pilot untied the plane from the dock and the back end of the floats went right under water. "That's quite a load you have there" he said. I hoped he wasn't going to remove anything, but he just climbed in and started her up. I guess if he was ok with it, it must be safe. And obviously it was or this would be a very short story.

Chugging his way to the south end of the lake, he turned the nose into the wind and without hesitation throttled up and the Beaver float plane started gaining speed, faster and faster, until the plane was skipping across the water. Finally the lake released her grip on the plane and I was flying. What a feeling! Climbing as he turned to the south west he straightened the plane onto his heading. Still climbing, the distant horizon became more and more distant. It was a relatively short trip of 40 minutes to my destination so I was curious "Why" I called to the pilot "Do you have to go so high when it is just a short trip". "Safety" was his reply "If we have engine trouble the higher we are the better our chance of coasting to a lake to land on" AHHHH… ok then… take her on up! But I was way too excited to be concerned about anything. Pointing out places on the flight like Nagagamisis Lake, the town of Hornepayne to the south and finally pointing straight ahead he yelled "Hiawatha Lake, where do you want to put down?"

Pointing to a spot on the western shore where a rock face met a nice sandy beach "Right there" I told him. And with that he banked to the left, circling the bay, looking for rocks or deadheads, anything really that might wreck his perfect landing record. At the southern most point of his second circle he leveled the plane and cut back the throttle. The beaver dropped like a rock! A few yards from the water the pilot gave her some fuel and brought the nose up as we skipped across the wave tops at high speed. Once close to the shore he cut back on the fuel and the floatplane settled nicely into the water.

Minutes later I was standing on the doorstep of my new home. With all my gear finally unpacked and piled on the shore the pilot unhooked the canoe and slid it into shore. I pulled it up on the beach and gave the plane a push out into the water. Starting his engine he taxied toward the south end of Hiawatha Lake. Lobo trotted down the hill, tail wagging as if to say, "This is going to be fun". I could not have agreed more.

CABIN BUILDING

(November 2)

The morning brought on cooler weather, so with a quick breakfast of oatmeal and coffee I got right to work. While setting the marten trap the night before, I had taken note of some good trees for building. Making my way back there, I fired up my axe and soon my first victim was lying on the ground. Measuring off an 18 and a 14 foot section, I cut the pieces off, trimming the branches as I went. Two more down! Another tree was a short distance away, and it was taken care of in the same manner.

With 4 more logs now I was ready to start bringing them to the building site to pile beside the others. There was no way I was going to carry all these logs so taking a rope I wrapped it around the smaller end of the log and tried dragging it. This was a lot easier than carrying the huge things. And after dragging a few of them it got even easier as I made a sort of trail with no sticks or grass to add resistance. But still, to get enough straight logs to make the cabin I would end up dragging them a quarter mile. That would take far more time than I had before winter set in.

But while looking around I did walk by my marten set and pick up my first piece of northern Ontario fur. A red squirrel had gotten itself caught in the # 120 conibear trap. I was in business! Deciding to have a coffee and think about this log issue, I made my way back to the fire and sat down. Apparently I think better with coffee.

The problem was that there was not enough logs close by to make the walls the height I needed. So I needed shorter walls. If I had more time I could eventually get enough trees to work with but for now… it struck me. Dirt walls! Sure, I had seen pictures of dugout cabins before. They were often built into a side hill, but why not a big hole with short wall around it. Thankfully I had included a spade in the list of tools to bring along.

Fetching the shovel I tested the soil where the cabin was to be. Under a one foot layer of blackish top soil was a nice clean sandy soil with a bit of consistency to it. Excited now I continued digging and finding only the odd small rock I made the decision. I would live in a hole in the ground for the winter.

For the next several hours I flung shovel load after shovel load out of the hole and into two piles that grew rapidly. Working the edge, as close as I could get to 12 feet by 14 feet in dimension I shoveled like I was applying for a grave diggers job. Finally I could stand it no more. I had to go check my traps. And hopefully set a few more. I had decided to at least spend a couple of hours a day trapping while the shelter was being built. After all you got to have some fun mixed in with all the work.

With the hole a good foot and a half deep all around I decided to cut another couple of trees and then head out. Not having to search for them now saved a little time, so at the first victim I put it on the ground in short order and in an hour had four more cabin logs ready to go.

Yes! I was off to check the traps! But, what about bait? I had a little pike left for one set but I needed more. There should be at least one beaver in my traps but that would not help until tomorrow. So it was up to my fishing rod to produce. Gathering what I needed, Lobo and I made our way to the canoe, jumped in and with a strong push we were off.

Straight across from the camp was the point that looked great for a mink and marten set. Landing there I hung a marten box in a tree about 50 feet in from the shore. Using the bait for this set I hoped for a good catch of fish for more sets. Getting the mink set all ready, a rock cubby guarded by a #1 victor longspring foot trap. Attached to a drown wire it was a very effective set. The mouth of the cubby should have about 1 to 2 inches of water at the entrance to cover the trap. Back in the canoe I pushed off from shore and got my fishing rod ready. I was not moving for more than a minute or two when WHAM... the rod almost flew out of the boat! Fumbling around I got control of it but whatever had hit it was gone.

Paddling smoothly along the shore I picked up a couple of pike and arrived at the beaver lodge with anticipation. I could see from the water that the slide set was not where it was supposed to be, and that was always a good sign. Beaching the canoe between a couple of big rocks Lobo beat me out to the lodge and my first check was the entrance set. It was sprung (probably by a rat) so moving to the other side I took hold of the wire and pulled up a nice big beaver.

Yes, marten bait! Resetting both traps I had a look at the mink cubby which was not touched. Just down from the house was a nice log with rat sign on it. From the canoe I cut out a notch just below the water level. With a fence staple and a length of wire, I attached a # 1 ½ foot trap, set it and placed it in the notch. Adding two more rat sets before the end of the river I looked for a likely spot to start the trail. This is where one of my main trails would leave the lake. To the east about a mile was a creek system that was made up of 9 small lakes over the course of about four miles. Hopefully there would be a lot of beavers in that area.

But for now I needed to get back to work so throwing in a mink set at the shore line I climbed the steep hill and came to the crest. Just like it was planned, there was a perfect white spruce right there to make my marten set on. Hanging the box and attaching the trap to a solid branch I turned and retraced my steps back down the hill. Back in the canoe I made a detour to the mouth of Hiawatha creek where it flowed out to Nagagami Lake, another perfect spot for a mink cubby. But seeing no flat rocks around I decided to use a marten box lying on the ground, with a # 120 in the entrance. Paddling back I trolled quite close to the beavers feed bed and picked up a small pike. It was probably after the minnows that always use the feed beds for cover. Before returning to camp I, of course added bait to the mink set on the point.

Having enough fish left for a late lunch/early supper I heated up a can of chili to go with it. Fit for a king it was! All it needed was a can of coke to wash it down. Now, back on the shovel, I started flinging dirt like there was gold under me. Who knows maybe there was? I never found it though. With a little over an hour before the sun disappeared I had a pretty good hole in the ground but there was one snag however, in the form of a big flat rock sticking out from the side of my wall. The more I dug the bigger this rock got. Leaning on the shovel for a moments rest (Yes, I felt like a government worker for a second), I thought to myself. That rock looks just like a coffee table. And you know... I must be magic, because that is exactly what it turned into, a nice rock table.

Wanting to use up the remainder of the day I grabbed my axe and since my compass was always in my pocket, I headed west with a slight southerly tilt to it. Blazing as I went, I stuck to my coordinates and was soon at the creek that my map had told me was there. Breaking out of the bush just at the north end of a beaver pond I was happy to see a nice big lodge with a huge feed bed in front of it. I would be back tomorrow to set this house and some marten traps. Hurrying back with Lobo I heard off in the distance the sound I had been waiting my whole life to hear, the sorrowful sound of timber wolves howling. To me, the true sound of the wilderness! Within seconds there were at least six different voices that I could pick out. Coming either from different directions or having a definite distinct sound. Oh how it thrilled me to hear this.

I listened for a few minutes until they had all located each other and went silent. Lobo let out a quiet growl, apparently, as I was to find out, he had no love for his distant cousins.

On the way back there was an explosion of wings as a ruffed grouse flew up. Darn I thought that would have been good for supper. To my surprise the bird landed in a tree just a short 100 feet away. Carefully lifting my 22 I took a shot. And missed! What the heck? The thing just sat there watching the dog. Inching closer it never even looked at me. Once I was within 20 feet I put a round through its head and supper was served. Fins and feathers tonight baby! Wait till the guys back home hear that you can walk right up to the grouse up here.

Back at camp, with a great meal (of which Lobo again got leftovers) in my belly I went about skinning my meager days catch. The squirrel was finished in minutes, held on the stretcher with four push pins. The beaver took more time and by the light of a Coleman lantern I removed its hide in about 20 minutes. With the practice I had gotten over the last few years I had become fairly adept at beaver skinning. Good enough that at the age of 16 I had placed 2nd, in a competition at a small local trappers rendezvous near Orillia.

Throwing the carcass outside I was happy that I now had enough bait to set a dozen plus marten traps. Finally, I climbed into my sleeping bag, turned the lantern to the off position and closed my eyes as the light slowly died. Lobo whined for a pat on the head, curled up at my feet and we both drifted off, the end to a most perfect day. Waking during the night Lobo had crawled outside to get some fresh air. Laying there wondering how my buddies Bill Clark and Don Wilson were doing on their trapline, I could feel the cold trying to pry its way into my sleeping bag. Huddling inside the sleeping bag I thought to myself "Better get that cabin finished buddy!"

(November 3)

Morning came in clear and cold. Shivering through breakfast I huddled close to the fire, enjoying a second cup of coffee. The first order of business was to hurry down the trail that I had blazed the night before and set up the beaver house and some marten sets. With traps and all my needed gear in the pack I took off at a brisk walk. It took only minutes to warm up and within an hour there were two more marten sets in and I was searching for the best spot to put my beaver traps. The dam had a perfect trail over it and that was always a great spot for a # 4 foot trap with a drown wire. Bedding the trap where the beavers had been climbing out to cross the dam I hammered a stake in and attached a wire long enough to reach a five foot depth. It took a few minutes to find a rock that weighed at least 20 pounds to use as an anchor. With a slide lock on the trap chain about 6 inches from the trap the beaver gets his foot caught, dives into the water and the lock and the anchor prevent him from surfacing. It takes mere minutes for him to expire.

The second set was a #330 conibear set on a trail where the beavers had been cutting trees for their feed bed. With that set completed I added a mink set below the dam. This was a bait hole set. Digging a 4 inch wide hole into the bank at the water line I placed a piece of bait at the back, about a foot into the bank, with a #1 foot trap in the entrance and a little mink scent on a stick inside the hole, a drown wire was added for a humane kill. Done and with that I hurried home to continue my cabin.

Back at camp again I jumped right on the shovel and by the time my stomach said it was lunch there was a hole on one end of the cabin that was at least 3 feet deep. Taking a quick lunch break I really had to convince myself not to go and check my traps at the south end of the lake. "No Dave" I told myself over and over "just work and then you can go check out the north end of the lake".

Holy Crap… only the third day in the bush and I was already arguing with myself. At least the dog wasn't being included in the argument. Pretty sure that sleeping by the fire was all he would have suggested. Shoot, forgot again to cut a dead tree on the way back from checking the traps. I would get one later on that evening, but for now it was back to the shovel. Hours later wanting a break from shoveling, I grabbed my axe and went to find another good tree for wall logs. Picking two, I knocked them down, limbed and cut them to size. Dragging one back, I again spent some time building my dirt piles.

As the day progressed and my arms grew four inches longer, impatience got the better of me. Finally relenting I grabbed my pack, threw in a few traps, a couple boxes and some bait and hurried to the water's edge. With Lobo by my side we climbed into the canoe and were off. The ease of paddling the sleek craft was a joy in comparison to the work of throwing dirt all day. With the end of the lake being less than two miles away I kept watch hoping to find another beaver house. Nothing! Although it was obvious why, there were very few poplar trees close enough to the water for the beavers to eat. They had literally eaten themselves out of house and home.

Finally, just inside a creek that flowed into Hiawatha Lake about a quarter mile from the north end, there was a dam holding back about three feet of water. Although I could not see a house, from the sign on the dam there was obviously one close by. And a dam set here would work great. With the nose of the canoe resting on the bottom of the dam, I told Lobo to get out. He just wagged his tail and stayed curled up, so stepping over him I went to exit the boat. That of course, is when Lobo decided that this was the time to make his move. Flying between my legs he sent me into a headlong dive into the frigid lake. You know the feeling when you do something really stupid and the first thing you do is look around to make sure no one noticed? YA!!! That's what I did. Not a person within 20 miles and I did the old head swivel to see if anyone was watching.

WHEW! I was in the clear. Nobody saw that splash. But hey! Thanks there dog. Keep up the good work. Climbing from the lake to the shore I went about setting the beaver trap, a #330 this time (it was faster than setting the drown wire set) because suddenly it seemed colder out. Next a rat trap went in on a floating log. Fifty feet down the shore I added a mink set and then I paddled to the very end of the lake. Here was where my main trail would leave the lake to join up with the Little Fraser River, and on to Ahmabel Lake. A hundred feet into the bush a marten set was added and I hurried back to paddle my way home.

The game warden in Hearst had told me that there was a moose hunting camp on Ahmabel Lake and that I would be able to stay there if I made it that far. Also they would normally leave a bunch of food in there when they left and I was welcome to it. That would be a big help once I made that trek.

It was getting to be dusk by then and I still wanted to get some work done on the hole/cabin. Paddling with a strong j-stroke the two miles were covered in under an hour having stopped only once, to set a mink trap at a promising looking spot. Back at the landing I realized that more firewood was needed so leaving Lobo there I paddled across to the point to check my two traps and bring a dead tree home with me. Pulling a nice buck mink from the drown wire set; I rushed to the marten box. Another squirrel! But wait, this was a Flying squirrel, you know like Rocky from the Bullwinkle show. They are not marketable so he went into the box for bait. Still no marten but at least I had my first mink. Should be a good 20 dollar bill! Taking one of the big dead spruce trees that lined the shore, it was cut it into manageable lengths and brought back to camp. At least the chopping had warmed me up some.

With no supper having been caught that day I dug into my store of supplies and mixed up a batch of bannock. There are lots of different recipes out there for bannock but mine was very simple.

A mixture of flour and baking powder with a little sugar added and placed in front of the open fire or fried in some lard on the stove. With jam or honey on it there was nothing better in the bush where bread was not available. Tempted to go and try to catch a fish first I knew that pike do not bite very well after dark, and, although I suspected that there were walleye in this lake, I had not caught any to this point.

So bannock and coffee it was. Cooking by the light of the fire I prepared the meal and after, with the mink dry, it was skinned out and the pelt put onto the stretcher. It was a gorgeous dark male that would bring a good buck for sure. Wondering, as I sat there, where the marten were hiding, I recalled hearing that they were not an intelligent animal. They had never developed a fear of traps or human odor, like most animals have. That was probably why they had almost been trapped out near the end of the last century. Conservation policies have brought them back to the numbers that we have today. With their main diet being mice, small birds and squirrels, I had read a study one time that stated that the Red Backed vole (a mouse that is abundant in the martens range) could make up to 80 % of its diet. Of course that number would go down as the snow got deep and the mice stayed under the snow cover.

And that struck a chord in my brain. Maybe they were not hungry enough to bother climbing the trees to investigate my sets. I would see what could be done do to make that easier for them. Flipping from the front to the back had gotten me dried off nicely. Throwing Lobo a beaver leg for his dinner, I climbed into my bedroll and with hands behind my head relaxed. It took a minute to realize what I was hearing. Snow flakes, falling on the tent. Too soon, snow was not needed already. I had really better get to work tomorrow. And fast!

Jolted awake at some point during the night by Lobo charging into the bush barking like a demon, I called him back and brought him into the tent. That was all I needed was to have the wolves (if that is what it had been) eat him during the night. Yes… I've read "White Fang". I know their tricks. Chuckling to myself, I was in no time, once again fast asleep.

(November 4)

Crawling from my sagging tent, I was met by a new world. It had turned white overnight! Starting a fire I decided to have a real good breakfast this morning. You start by frying a potato sliced up thin, when they are done you take half a can of Klik (or Spam, same stuff) and fry it sliced up. When it is done you move it all to the side and pour in a half can of creamed corn. Once heated you have a delicious three course breakfast. This had been a favorite meal of mine when on canoe trips in Algonquin Park just north of Huntsville, Ontario. I had made sure to bring a modest supply of both Klik and the creamed corn.

While waiting for my meal to cook, I wondered if there were any tracks from whatever Lobo had freaked on last night. Taking my coffee I took a quick stroll behind camp and sure enough, there half covered by the snow were tracks. Not of wolves but a big moose had wandered by during the night. Being close to the marten set, I went to check on it. Nothing hanging but there were marten tracks at the base of the tree. Darn! A running pole, that's it. I would put a leaning pole at all the sets to hopefully make it easy enough that they may try for the bait.

Hurrying back before my food burnt I was excited now. Maybe this would get some action. Also since the set still had fish for bait I would come back and refresh the set with beaver. Back at the fire my meal was thoroughly enjoyed before starting work. Once finished with breakfast the shovel and I had another go around and did some serious dirt moving. Nothing like a shot of winter to motivate a guy! Back on the shovel, by late afternoon there was a hole that was four feet deep and eight feet long. The front half of the cabin was 18 inches deep and on the right side I left it like that as my sleeping area and to the left the floor had a gradual slope down to the living area.

With that done it was time to start on the log walls. There was 8 logs cut and at the site, so they were put in place, notching the bottom of each log to fit snuggly over the log underneath it. Never notch the top of the bottom log because water will settle in the notch and rot the logs. With all eight logs in place I figured that there would be eight more needed to make the roof high enough so I would be able to stand upright inside. As I worked Lobo came up as if to say "let's go hunting". Darn he almost talked me into it again. That dog was a bad influence.

Pole after pole I dragged, sawing, notching and chopping until there was a nice wall three feet high. Wait, I needed a door! With that thought I cut a 3 foot wide opening in the front wall of the cabin. Taking a couple of logs six inches thick and about 4 feet long I sawed and chopped until there was two flat boards about the size of a 2 by 6 stud. Nailing them as a door frame to hold the cut logs in place, I then added another log to each end of the structure. Will the roof poles be strong enough to hold the weight of the dirt I was going to throw on top? I didn't think so. A ridge pole across the middle for support was needed. Removing the two end logs that had just been put in place I cut one more 16 foot log and heaved it into its spot. Some notching and replacing of the two end logs got the cabin ready for the roof poles. But something was still bothering me.

Looking around I tried to figure out what it was. Suddenly, spying my woodstove it hit me. A stove pipe hole! Off came the back log again as I disconnected my saw blade, sliding it through the space between the second and third log down. Reattaching the blade to the bow I cut a one foot section out of the log. Now the structure was ready for the roof poles. But with not much daylight left I decided that was enough for today and some traps needed checking.

The south end of the lake was beckoning me so all my gear went into the canoe and the dog was left on shore whining. I pushed off and slid easily through the water heading east. As the canoe scraped the rocky shore where my first two traps were set I hurried to the marten trap. Darn! Same deal, tracks but no marten. Adding a running pole quickly I looked in the mink cubby and the trap was gone. Good enough. A mink will do fine. Pulling the wire I was surprised to see my first marten attached to the foot trap. Right on, but this was not the beautiful fine furred animal that I had seen at the Trappers Convention in North Bay. This looked like a drowned rat. But it was still my first marten!

Pumped now I hurried down the lake, trolling along the way and probably a little too fast because I never even got a nibble. Arriving at the lodge another beaver plus two rats and a squirrel were added to my catch. Not bad for the number of traps that had been checked. Taking my time paddling back I picked up a good eight pound Northern that put up a good fight. But he was bested and supper was in the boat. Back at the landing Lobo came sauntering down the hill, apparently unimpressed with the days catch. Well the heck with you, dog!

Hauling everything up the hill I got ready to cook supper. Fish and... potatoes it was! With coffee in hand, I sat back and studied my progress. A couple days work at the most would have the cabin finished. If I went and set a bunch of traps tomorrow, then they could do their thing while the finishing touches were put on my new home. Sounded good to me! But with not enough bait to make a lot of sets I decided that the beaver that was just caught needed to be skinned. Either now or early in the morning and since I really wanted to get an early start, now got the vote.

A half an hour later I was in bed, and I must have been tired because I blinked once and that blink lasted a good eight hours.

A DAY OF EXPLORATION

(November 5)

Dawn found me at the north end of Hiawatha Lake checking my beaver trap. With a nice beaver in it the trap was reset and fifty feet away added a mink to my fur bag. It had been dark when I went by the other mink set so it would be checked on the way home. Beaching the canoe at the Little Fraser River trail head, I threw my pack on my shoulders, picked up the two marten boxes that would not fit in my pack and started off. With an occasional look at my compass I passed my marten set, removed the flying squirrel and kept on my north heading, blazing every 30 feet or so. At approximately the halfway mark I set one of the marten boxes with a running pole included this time. Carrying on over fallen trees, around large boulders, through grassy swales until finally I saw ahead of me what had to be the opening for the river.

I made another set there, because I figured the marten would travel the edge of this open area looking for food and my trap would be waiting for them. I had noticed marten tracks a half dozen times in the last mile since I had left Hiawatha Lake, and that was a good sign, lots of animal movement. Just before we broke out into the open Lobo jumped a family of grouse. But these were different. I had seen pictures of these before, spruce grouse, apparently the dumbest birds on the planet, next to the dodo bird. And we all know what happened to them. I shot two of them with my 22, and the other three just sat there staring. Maybe they would be around on my next trip.

The river was nothing more than a creek at this point. Being able to walk across it almost anywhere, I did just that and moved on downstream. A short distance away was a rifle where the creek split around a rocky sand bar. The snow on the sandbar was covered with tracks. Otters! And right at what looked like a perfect spot to set two traps. Blocking the water on each side of the sandbar, until it was narrow enough for a #330 conibear, I placed the traps and anchored them solidly to a stake hammered into the ground. With a little grass over the traps for concealment I was satisfied. I just hoped the otters would be happy with it also.

Just down from that set the river opened up quite a bit. From here as far as I could see was a wide grassy field with the river winding its way through it. At one point it came very close to the bush line that I was walking along so I set a mink trap on an old beaver house right on the curve. In the bush at the same place I made a marten set. With just one more box with me I waited until I found a beaver house to set and placed it there. Moving on I didn't even realize I had just passed one of the best otter sets you will find, a dead beaver house. The entrances are usually very easy to find and otters love to investigate them. But I did not know that back then. Every so often I would find a log that I was able to drop a rat trap on. I would cut a long stick, blaze it and stick it into the ground to mark the spot.

One thing I had noticed though was that there was very few poplar trees here just like along Hiawatha Lake. They had all been cleared far back into the bush and the beavers had moved on, following the food. It was not long after that the water started getting deeper. From a distance I noticed a lodge sticking up out of the grassy meadow. A new dam was holding the water back but like most new dams there was no established trail over the top, so I had opted to make a couple of feed trail sets. Adding the last marten box that was with me, I moved on hoping to find another beaver lodge before I got to my scheduled turn around point, a small lake about 5 miles from where I had left my canoe.

Finally, the lake was in front of me. My stomach was telling me that it was way past lunch time so after building a fire I set a can of beans at the edge of the flames to warm up. Stirring occasionally as they started to bubble it gave me time to ponder. One live house in this stretch of river was pretty poor. But where there is no food there will be no beavers. I gazed out on this beautiful little lake, bare rock shores dropping off right into the water which was a deep blue, almost black color. It made me wonder if there were any fish in here. The lake was only a half mile long with another creek flowing in just to the north of my position. That would be explored on my next trip down this way.

My beans were boiling and I was wishing for a hot coffee, but I contented myself with a drink of ice cold water. As I was bent over drinking I heard, coming from the lake a half bark half coughing noise. What the heck was that? I looked out but saw nothing. That's odd. I turned back to my beans and there it was again. Spinning, I saw four round whiskery faces bobbing up and down in the lake. Otters! One barked and they all disappeared, only to come back up a few yards away. Again and again they carried on with this game. I enjoyed the show as I ate my lunch and before I turned back for home I named this spot Otter Lake. I made a last mink set on the lake shore and headed back to camp. Leaving what traps I had left hanging in a tree for my return made it a bit of a lighter carry back.

Hurrying back I picked up my two spruce grouse and to my surprise there was a gorgeous marten in the trap that I had just set a few hours earlier. Right on! By the time I reached Hiawatha Lake it was dark, again. Paddling back I checked the mink set and it had not been touched. A flock of whistlers sailed overhead to land in the bay off to my left. Holdouts, or just really slow fliers, they were the only ducks I had seen since being dropped off on the 1st. Pulling up to the landing I looked up and the stars were so bright it was like I could reach up and grab one. Again I thought of my friends and wondered how trapping was going for them. I would have bet that they had more fur at this point, considering the main HWY # 17 ran right through the middle of their trap line. But I knew that they were not having as much fun as I was.

It had been a long day so with a good meal of spruce grouse and bannock, I relaxed with a cup of coffee and stared into the fire, drifting back in time to my days of trapping near the Severn River, catching beavers, rats, coon, mink, fox and the odd coyote. Times where school chums would want to come and see what trapping was all about. Like when Dave (fartin) Martin came in and as he stumbled his way across a beaver dam that I had practically run across, he shouted out "look at that bush rabbit go". For the next 2 years that name stuck and I had my first and last nickname of my life. It died when I moved north. Funny hey, I never told anyone that was my nickname.

With a smile at the memory, I said goodnight to Lobo, crawled into my bed and without a blink I was asleep.

CABINS FINISHED

(November 6)

With sunlight hitting me in the eyes, I stretched and crawled my way from my bed to the tent door. As my food was cooking and the coffee water was heating, I made an attack plan for the day. A short distance down the lake shore was a stand of young black spruce. They were all very near the same size and would make perfect roof poles. The dog would have to stay at camp since I planned on filling the canoe with poles and it would take several trips. Finally with the last mouthful of coffee sliding down my throat I headed off, axe in hand. Breaking a little ice on the shore I piled into the canoe and a short five minute paddle brought me to the spruce stand.

For several hours I chopped down, limbed and trimmed off the top of the 60 or so poles that I would need to cover the roof. With an average of about 4 inches at the big end each pole did not cover much space. When there was, what I hoped was enough I started hauling them into the canoe and back to camp. Needing to be at least 14 feet long I laid them on the roof, each one opposite the other. One butt end pointing to the north, and the next to the south and soon enough I had them all in place and was short by 3. One more trip and I was finished with this job.

Now to make sure there were no stubs of branches sticking up that would puncture the plastic lining that would be between the poles and the dirt. Making sure that the poles were smooth, I decided to have some lunch and start shoveling soon after.

With one grouse breast left from last night and a can of chili, I had a fantastic lunch. I even mixed up some of my tiny supply of Tang to go with it. God… seriously, could it get any better than this! With lunch finished I placed the plastic sheet on the roof, tacking the edges down with a few roofing nails. Next, I proceeded to start moving the pile of dirt on to the top of the plastic. Before I piled too much dirt I remembered to cut a support pole for the main beam and installed it inside the cabin. Finished with that I started moving dirt in earnest. Barely 2 hours later, I had a good 4 inch layer of soil over the entire roof. That should be good insulation.

Climbing on to the roof I leveled it all evenly and surveyed my handy work. It was good! Back on the ground I took my airtight heater (a tin woodstove used commonly in trappers cabins) and the stove pipes and went inside to set it up. After finding some rocks to lift the stove about 4 inches, because someone (Lobo) had forgotten to measure the length of the stove pipe, I had a working heat source. This was going great, not even near dark yet and the cabin was all but finished. Maybe I could sleep in an actual building tonight. That would be so cool!

Grabbing some firewood I tossed it all inside and followed it in to get a fire going. As the stove heated up, the protective coating of paint burnt off filling the cabin with a smelly smoke. It soon cleared out however and I was soon enough hauling all my supplies into the structure. Finally I could get the stretched furs dry, as they had been just sort of hovering between dry and wet up until this point. With a limited amount of stretchers getting the furs to dry in a couple days would be imperative. With the last bit of light I shoveled sand all around the base of my camp and packed it in tight. Tomorrow I would bring some moss back with me to chink the walls between the logs. Throwing my entire supply of firewood into the cabin I then decided to go and get some more. It was sort of dark but I could still see well enough with the moon to cut a tree and haul it back with me. Bucking it up and adding it to the pile inside took but an hour. Now supper was needed and bad. I should have spent some time out on the lake looking for a fish or two to supplement my meager food supply. Ya and if frogs had wings they wouldn't bump their ass when they hopped too! Shoulda, woulda, coulda, I guess it would be Irish stew and bannock for supper. After eating I worked long into the night making my cabin more comfortable. A shelf here, some nails along the ridge pole to hang the stretchers. Level off and smooth out my bedding area and store everything in its proper place. The back half of the cabin was great with about six and a half feet of clearance, but the front was only about four and a half feet high.

Good enough to sleep in and store things so it would work out fine. Opening a box that had been hidden in my tent I found the thermometer that I had brought and my transistor radio that I had forgotten all about. With only one spare battery I promised myself to play the radio only 30 minutes a night. Also in there was my book that I had intended to use as a journal. I would spend some time tonight catching up on my entries while I enjoyed some radio. The air was turning colder and as I crawled outside to answer Mother Nature's call, I felt snowflakes landing on my face. Great, I would be able to see fresh tracks in the morning.

Off in the distance I heard the wolves howling again and this time the crazy dog joined in. Sure announce your location to them so they can come and eat you. Stupid dog! He wanted nothing to do with the heat that the woodstove was producing so leaving him outside I slid a beaver stretcher in front of the opening to act as a door. Back inside I planned out my next days adventures. Excited that the cabin was finally finished, I could now get trapping in earnest. Tomorrows plan was to travel to the south end of the lake and blaze the trail to the Chain Lakes, as I had come to call the system to the east of Hiawatha.

With a last coffee in hand, the radio playing songs from the Kapuskasing radio channel and me recording the happenings so far, I soon found myself drifting off to sleep. OK! The radio went off and the light out. It was going to be a long day tomorrow.

(November 7)

Waking, the first thing I noticed was the morning light creeping through the cracks in my cabin walls. This would be different from now on. In the tent the sunlight always announced wake up time. But now it would be dark and my brain would tell me to keep sleeping. I should have brought an alarm clock. Oh well, I guess l would get up late some days. Not like I was on a schedule or I was going to get a warning slip for being late.

Flipping the draft on the stove and opening the damper on the stove pipe, the fire was roaring in seconds. I had filled the stove with wood last night and then shut all the openings down. The wood had smoldered all night waiting for that first blast of air to bring it to life. The mink, rats and squirrel pelts were drying nicely so I moved them back but the beavers needed a little more time. As my meal was cooking I turned the marten pelts inside out by pushing the nose back through the mouth and rolling it like a sock. You have to be careful that the skin is not to dry because it can tear as you do this. You also have to make sure that it is not to green or it will stick to the drying board. Even with a belly stick, they are hard to remove if that happens.

Marten, fox, lynx, wolves, coyotes and fisher pelts are all sold with the fur on the outside. This is because the fur can vary so much in color and the buyers need to see this. Rats, mink, otter, coon, squirrels and weasels are sold fur side in. This is so the hide can be seen easily for damages. The fur color can be judged by checking the area at the base of the tail. And in the case of mink and otter it protects the fur from being touched which can cause "singging".

This is when the end of the hairs curl or split and it drastically reduces the value of the pelt. Beavers are skinned open. That means you slice up the belly from the bottom lip to the tail and stretch the hide in an oval.

As the coffee pot started to boil, I mixed up a cup and readied my food. With breakfast finished I grabbed my Woods # 1 packsack and crawled through the doorway. YIKES! There was a good 4 inches of snow on the ground. I spun, already knowing the answer. Yup, my tent was flattened. Oh well I would deal with that later, for now I had traps to set and trails to explore. Filling my pack with traps and the gear I needed to set them I strolled down to the lake.

The canoe was full of snow and frozen into the ten feet of ice that lined the shore. I guess I now know to pull the canoe out and flip it over for the night. Live and learn. Cleaning out the canoe, I loaded the dog, pack, gun and myself in and pushed off from shore. The ice tried to hold me there but I pushed through it and into the open water. As I headed across the lake to my sets on the point the waves slapped against the side of my canoe sending the spray up and onto Lobo. He wasn't that impressed.

At the point, I picked up a nice marten in the box set but the mink trap was sprung and the bait gone. It must have been set off before the snow because there were no tracks around. Rebaiting the set, I turned south and I let the wind push me as I tried picking up a fish for supper. To no avail however, and upon reaching the beaver house I found a rat in the entrance set and a small beaver in the slide set. That was three beaver out of this house so I pulled the traps and carried on down the river.

By the time I reached my Chain Lakes trail head I had added a small female mink and two more rats to the catch. It was nice to get the rats because once the ice was in, the rat catching would be done. I realized I had gone right past the mink set at the beaver house. Ok I'll catch it on the flip side. At the start of the trail I wondered if there was a marten waiting for me at my last trap of the day. Climbing the hill, I reached the top and yes... or no. It was just a Red Squirrel. Still counted as a pelt though!

Stepping past the trap I was again travelling new territory. The rush I always got from seeing new ground was something that I hoped would never go away. With every step I wondered to myself, "Has any person ever stepped here before"? It was a neat feeling in this day and age, where there are not too many places left where a guy can even wonder that. With my compass out I moved through the bush quite quickly, not bothering to blaze the trail. With the fresh snow on the ground I could follow my tracks back and reroute the trail at points if needed. The blazing could be done then.

I dropped a box at approximately the halfway point and then another as the lake opened up to me. Cool not 100 feet from where I hit the lake was a beaver lodge with a real nice feed bed. That meant there should be lots of beavers here with this much feed put in. Beavers keep their young with them for two years so if there has been no predation by wolves, bear or otters then there could be up to ten in a house. I have trapped houses where the feed was so good there were several families on a pond. I would imagine they were all part of an original family. These beaver would almost definitely be all scarred up from fighting with each other.

But too much food is not something any of the beavers up here had to deal with. That was for sure. Making two quick sets, one an entrance and the other a beaver run, which is a tunnel that the beavers dig into a bank as a place to eat in safety and a place where they can go for air in the fall when the ice locks up the surface of the water. Beside the beaver house I put in a mink cubby and headed north to where the creek emptied into the lake. Setting a marten trap between Lake 3 and Lake 4, I found that # 4 was a dry pond, so I continued through the grass to Lake 5. There I found a small house that looked like it only had a new couple living there.

Not bothering to set that one, I kept going. Between 5 and 6 I put in my last marten box and found what looked to me like a perfect otter set. The creek narrowed down at one point to about 18 inches wide and a foot deep. With a # 330 conibear blocking any swimming animal from going any further I added a few sticks to guide them into my trap, anchored it to a stake in the ground and I was done. Hey it looked good to me. If I was an otter I would swim through there.

With no more marten boxes to set I continued on exploring and blazing the new trail. All this time Lobo would follow behind, curl up in the snow while I set traps and follow again as I started moving. Must be boring being a dog! The map showed a half mile of creek between Lake 6 and 7. It was a wide shallow creek with maybe 4 inches of water over mud. As I walked through the grass lining the water I looked up and there stood my first moose out in the wild. Oh my god! This thing was huge! The antlers looked like they were five feet across. He watched us and we watched him. He seemed far less impressed with me than I was with him but Lobo just looked at it like he had seen them every day.

Finally the show was over and we both continued on our way. What a sight! With the day two thirds gone I figured now would be a good time to head for home. Dropping in a couple of rat sets as I moved south I reached Lake 3 and turned west Following my tracks, blazing as I went I detoured around a few thick spots but eventually had a good trail. Breaking out of the bush at Hiawatha we piled into the canoe and I back paddled out from shore.

Remembering to check the mink trap which held nothing I dropped a lure in the water and slowly dragged it behind as we made our way home. Two northern, one close to six pounds, were added to the days catch. The fur was kind of shabby on them but they sure would eat fine.

Back in my cabin after a long day, I hung the animals up and made a coffee. Outside I skinned the marten and squirrel before checking into my tent. It was ripped from the snow in a few places but nothing that could not be fixed, so I cleared all the snow off it and pushed it into the cabin to hang and dry. Needing to cut some firewood at every opportunity I grabbed my axe and made my way down the hill. There were a lot of trees to the right of my landing so I walked down the shore and dropped a good sized one. Dragging it back with me, I did my best impression of Paul Bunyan and it was stacked neatly on the pile in no time.

With supper as my next chore I made some more bannocks and used a cornmeal coating for the fish. With a little sugar added to the bannock mix it made it that much better but the cornmeal fish was not a success. I decided to stick with the flour coating from now on. Once my meal was finished I started on the rats and the mink, hoping that the beaver would be dry enough to skin when I was finished with the little critters. An hour later I was and so was he. Thirty minutes after that the beaver was on the board, nailed into a perfect oval, and scraped clean on the plywood stretcher.

Skinning what I could outside, (which would not last long) and using the woodstove to cook with was helping to conserve my meager supply of lantern fuel. But not fast enough. I would have to figure another lighting system or learn to cook and basically live in the dark. The fuel needed to be saved for skinning. I would have to think on that problem but for now I just needed to get some sleep. Opening my bedroll I lay there wondering how the little baby had fared, hoping that everything had turned out o.k. I turned on the radio for a few minutes to listen to the sounds of Kapuskasing, and woke up awhile later to turn it off. Two breaths later I was asleep again as I had visions of animals diving into my traps. Tomorrow would tell!

NORTHWARD BOUND

(November 8)

Coffee on, breakfast cooking and the pack all set to head out. I was anxious to head north and check my traps along the Little Fraser river trail. A solid breakfast of Klik, potatoes and creamed corn with a chunk of bannock to boot should hold me till my return. Other than a piece of the bread replacement I was carrying no food with me today. I would not have the time to stop and cook anything anyway.

There were only seven marten boxes left and so I would need to spread them out quite a bit. I used another set that I had thought might work once the boxes were all in trees. I brought four with me and saved the last three for the Pody Lake trail tomorrow.

Looking at the empty Klik can I had an idea, but it could wait till I got home that evening. Downing my last mouth full of coffee I headed out the door. With the thermometer reading right around the freezing mark I noticed that the lake was dead calm. Throwing everything into the canoe, Lobo piled in and I followed. With no wind to hamper my progress the canoe moved effortlessly through the water.

Being in a hurry I didn't even wet a lure on the trip that morning. Moving this fast, it would be a waste of time anyway. Covering the two miles to the beaver set I removed a rat from the beaver trap, and reset the sprung muskrat trap. Nothing in my mink sets either, so I moved down the short distance to my trail and pulled up on shore.

Wolf tracks covered the shore line and followed my trail into the bush. Lobo sniffed the tracks and emitted a low warning growl. I took that as a sign that the tracks were quite fresh. Loading up all the gear I headed off, following the wolves right to my first set. There a big beautiful dark marten was waiting for me. The wolves had come right up and checked it out but thankfully did not touch it. My next set was sprung with a little bit of fur left in the trap. It looked like flying squirrel fur and a marten had come and eaten it. My last set before the river produced a big buck mink. So they would climb a little too if they were curious enough.

Something I was starting to notice, I wasn't sure if it was the running poles or the fact that now with the snow deeper, and it was harder for them to catch mice so they were coming to the bait better. Whatever the reason I was happy that the marten were finally cooperating. Another great start and it could only get better. Anxious to check my first ever otter trap I hurried to the creek and from twenty feet away I could see that one of the traps was not where I placed it. Real excited now I grabbed the wire and loved the heavy feeling as I pulled it out of the water. A big flat scaly tail broke the surface first. Darn, just a beaver.

But what was he doing here? I was almost a mile from the closest beaver house downstream. Checking how the trap was set I realize that he had come from upstream. There must be a house close by to the west. Cool, I would check for it on the way home. Moving downstream, I checked trap after trap picking up two rats and then another marten. Arriving at the beaver house I was rewarded with a medium beaver and a sprung trap.

As I walked I was amazed at the number of moose track that there were wandering through the meadows. Along with fox, marten and mink tracks I came upon the tracks of a pack of wolves once

I got close to Otter Lake where I had turned around on my last trip. They proceeded to follow my tracks and at both mink sets they sprung the traps and stole the bait. Maybe on my next trip I would have to try and teach them a lesson. Snares should be good for that! Just in from the lake shore I hung a marten box in a tree and worked at readying the set.

Picking up my trap cache I moved along the lake shore until I came to the creek that flowed in from a series of two lakes that I was hoping would have some beavers in them. Placing a mink set near the creek between the first Otter Lake and the first of the new lakes, I arrived to find a house that probably was alive last year. Hopefully they had moved to the next lake upstream. Setting one of my last two boxes between these lakes I came out to a very pretty little lake. And the prettiest thing about it was the giant beaver house on the west shore.

Marten tracks in the bush and mink and otter all around the creek made me excited to be setting this area. Putting in a mink set on the back side of the dam I used a #120 conibear trap instead of the foot trap because there was not enough water for a drowning set. And I figured that the water would be frozen soon anyway. Setting a slide and a trail set took no time at all and I just hoped that something would get caught before the ice moved in. Behind the house I made a different marten set. Cutting a pole about twenty feet long with the small end being about three inches wide , I wired it to a standing tree so that the last six feet were hanging past the main tree and the end was about six feet of the ground. Then nailing a small stick, about six inches long by an inch wide across the pole at about one foot from the end and squeezed a # 220 onto the small cross stick. Finally a bait piece got nailed to the very end of the pole and the whole thing was covered with a thick layer of spruce boughs. Lastly the trap was wired to the main running pole. The boughs were to keep birds off the bait and to make it look like the only way into the bait was to go through the trap opening. Thinking that it would be nice to have some scent to put on the log I decide to try and make some at home. Deciding that this was as far as I would go till freeze up (I did not know where the cabin on Ahmabel Lake was, and walking all the way around the shore line didn't interest me at all), I turned back for home.

Wanting to look for the colony that the beaver had come from I hurried on and picked up my fur along the way. About halfway back I came across the tracks of the wolves again. There had been five in the other pack and this one had only four but I was sure it was the same group. The other one must have wandered off for a bit. A quarter mile further down the trail a single wolf track crossed my trail. This was a big animal, his tracks probably five inches across. He must be scouting ahead for some prey I imagined.

At the spot where my trail turned south toward Hiawatha Lake I dropped my pack and with my axe in one hand and two traps in the other I headed west along the creek. Thinking that the lodge should be close by I was amazed that I travelled nearly a half mile before the bush opened up and I had me another house to set. With a nice trail over the dam I made a set there and then another in a bank run. Two fast, easy and productive sets; my three favorite components in a trap set. Backtracking to my pack I hefted it up onto my shoulders and moved south.

As I moved toward the lake it seemed that the temperature was falling and the wind started picking up. The trees were moving pretty good anyway. Lobo let out a whine and I agreed. It was time to get back as the sun was fading fast. Stopping only to shoot a Ruffed Grouse, I arrived at the lake where my suspicions were confirmed, the lake was a white, wind whipped mess. Hurrying we boarded the canoe and pushed off. Hugging the west shore to stay out of the northwest wind we had no trouble until I had to enter the narrows. Here with the lake being barely sixty yards wide, the waves had built in the narrow confines.

Navigating through with nothing more than a few waves joining us in the canoe we entered the narrows and had clear sailing back to camp.

Again arriving at camp with no light in the sky, not even stars were out tonight with the heavy cloud cover that had moved in. Oh well, I never was one to be afraid of the dark so why let it bother me now.

Everything into the camp and all the animals hung to dry left me with but one chore. You know it! Supper! A wonderful meal of grouse, boiled potatoes and green beans… Oh Yummy! Filleting the breast meat off the bird I threw the rest to Lobo. The grouse are so much better up here where I can put a bullet through their head instead of wing shooting them and filling the meat full of pellets, feathers and blood.

With supper finished and my skinning taken care of, I fell into bed exhausted. That of course is when Mother Nature would call. Maybe she was sending me a warning because stepping outside I noticed big snowflakes falling. The wind had died right down too, and looking at the thermometer the temperature was now down to 22 degrees farenheight. Since I was outside already I grabbed my flashlight and went to check my backyard marten trap. Ya Baby! A big male marten! The end to another perfect day and I couldn't wait to see what tomorrow would bring!

IT'S SNOW TIME

(November 9)

SNOW !!! That's what tomorrow brought me. Snow and ice! Enough snow that I could barely see my tracks from last night. Walking to the lake to fill my water pail I looked out onto a new world. One with a lake covered in ice. I guess they were right, any time after the 7th. Stepping to the edge of the ice I slid myself out a couple of feet and stomped my foot. Nothing! One more time I moved out a step or two and tried again, harder this time. All that got me was reverberations running up my leg. Ok, back to get my axe.

Returning, I took a couple swings and made it through. The top ice was solid but underneath the snow had formed a kind of slushy ice that should freeze up good and thick with this cold weather. But for now it was not safe to walk on. That was ok because I was heading down the Pody Lake trail today. I wanted to set my last three marten boxes down that way and see what other sets I could make. My intentions were to follow the creek from where my two beaver sets were, down to where it emptied into a long skinny lake that I was going to call Little Pody Lake. Looking at the map I had noticed that both lakes had almost identical shapes with Pody running north to south and Little Pody running west to east. Pody was probably five times the size of his little brother.

After chopping the hole and filling the pail I hefted it up to the cabin and set about filling my belly. Not being in too much of a hurry, as this trip should only take half a day or so, I relaxed with a coffee as my meal was cooking. With my belly full I finally started gathering all the gear I would need for the days trip. With traps, wire, pliers, snares, bait and my trusty axe along with my 22 which, by the way, I was starting to get sick of dragging around with me everywhere, I started off down the trail behind my camp. These were the conditions that I disliked the most. The snow was too deep for easy walking, your feet would slip as you tried to push off, and it would tighten up your hamstrings something awful. It was also not deep enough for snowshoes yet. I couldn't wait till I was able to break out my "shoes" for travelling.

Now that my canoeing days were finished the daily walks just got that much further, and having the 22 with me would get old real fast. I had not seen a furbearer that I could shoot with it anyway, but it was sure nice to have fresh grouse every once in awhile. So for now it would come with me and I would make the decision later to stop bringing it along. To this point I had not even taken my Winchester Model 70 30-06 out of its case. I had thought of maybe shooting a moose to have meat for the winter, but after seeing that giant bull the other day, I honestly wouldn't have had a clue what to do with it. I would have hated to kill something like that and let any of it go to waste.

Finally on the trail with Lobo in tow I passed the trap that had yielded the marten last night and moved on. Again I was amazed by the number of tracks that could appear in such a short time after the snow. Marten, weasel, a fox and everywhere the squirrel tracks. At my second trap was a squirrel that would however never make another track. With a beaver in each set and a marten in the last trap, I pulled the one set, leaving the dam set in. It would still be effective because I broke a hole in the dam and put the trap in deeper water. Hopefully an otter or beaver would use the opening to try and get over the dam.

Pulling the foothold trap set for mink I made a few adjustments and soon had the cubby guarded by a #120 conibear. I really should have pulled both beaver traps but I really needed the meat both for bait and for Lobo food. I rationalized it by calling it an otter set now. See, change a couple words around and everything is good. Moving along I placed the three marten boxes at good looking locations as I went, kind of following the creek from a little ways off. This creek was now flowing through a huge Black Spruce area. Heavily moss covered ground that had built up on the root systems of the trees which made for difficult walking. Knowing from my map that this stream would take me directly to Little Pody Lake I had not even taken my compass out of my pocket.

Blazing as I went, the trail wound along, by passing thick sections, around large deadfalls and generally trying to stay into the more open bush, little though there was of it. Finally the bush opened up and a beaver pond presented itself to me. In the center of the pond I could see a large white lump. I could still see feed sticking up through the snow so there must have been a good size pile there.

With the house being out in the middle of the pond and any trails frozen over I decided to make a dam gateway set. This set is made by cutting a narrow hole in the ice about six inches wide and maybe eight feet long straight out from the dam. Then you start gathering sticks, poles and a small Spruce tree. Pushing the poles and sticks down into the mud along the hole in the ice you block the entire area off, with the Spruce tree going at the very end. At the point where the water is about 18 inches deep you take a #330 and slide a two inch pole through the spring holes and take the sticks out that are blocking that spot. Setting the trap into that opening, you should catch every beaver that swims along checking on his dam.

From the dam I could see the opening that must be Little Pody Lake only a hundred yards away. Heading that way I suddenly spotted a little brown face poking out of the snow. A mink! Leveling my 22, I took aim and... he was gone. Oh there he is, popping up several yards away, but gone again before I can get the sights on him. We play this game for a few minutes till he tires of it and then just disappears. Well I guess I might as well make a mink set close by here. On the shore of the lake I checked as best I could for a lodge and not seeing anything I decided to head back and get some work done. I could use the daylight to cut some Birch for fire wood and save some lantern fuel by skinning outside.

I also wanted to try out my fuel saving light invention that I had been thinking about. Lobo spooked up a flock of Grouse and shooting two I watched the others fly off. Seeing where one had landed I went after it and got that one also. Great, I'll have a nice supper for the next couple of days. I may even try making some jerky with some of the meat. Back at camp with another big load I did my regular chores and added in a couple of hours of cutting firewood. I am not used to being at camp with this much daylight left. While retrieving a pail of water I again checked the ice. Still too soft to travel on, and with the temperature hanging around the freezing mark it was not going to get much better.

The rest of the daylight was used to skin my catch and slice all the fat off the beaver carcasses. Inside now, for the night, I put the frying pan on the stove and filled it with the beaver fat. Rummaging through the garbage I found the empty Klik cans that I had finished with. Slicing a one inch hole in the lid I slid a ten inch piece of my spare lamp wick (my snowshoe harnesses were made by Bates and were attached to the shoes with one inch lamp wick) through the hole in the can. Once the fat had been rendered down, I filled the bottom of the can and put the two halves together again. In no time the oil had seeped up the lamp wick and I lit it. IT WORKED! It gave off enough light to work by but not enough to be able to skin with. But at least I could keep the lantern off now when I wasn't skinning.

Going through the garbage again I made another lamp to keep near my bed. Later that night I discovered that the lamps had to be kept warm or the oil would turn semi-solid and not travel up the wick. So every so often I would set it on the stove and the flame would slowly increase. "Well that was a success, hey dog" I said to Lobo. He waged a "Ya, whatever you say Boss" and went back to sleep.

That sounded like a good idea so with a coffee in hand I hit the sack to listen to some bed side music all the way from Kapuskasing. And since it was the only station I could receive, I thought it was a phenomenal radio station. With my allotted time for the radio used up I rolled over blew out the light and watched the smoke curl up as the light died. With the radio off I could hear the sounds from outside again.

Lobo was whining and the wolves were howling. Close by! Pulling the door aside I called the dog in and trapped him inside and safe. Back I drifted, into a dream filled sleep where martens abound and I never caught a worthless Flying squirrel.

(November 10)

My first thought after my eyes opened was, "Did it get cold over night"? Sliding the door open I did not even need to look at the thermometer to know. It had actually warmed up. I could see water dripping from the branches. Not even bothering to go out I just left the door wide open for light and made myself a cup of Java. Over breakfast I decided that today would be camp day. Clean up and cut firewood all day. Not that cutting firewood was boring; but yes it was! Compared to checking traps, it was mind numbing.

Fighting the urge to go check Chain Lakes, my common sense prevailed and I stayed put. The wood pile grew substantially and by afternoon I decided that I needed to go for a walk. Back down the trail to Little Pody where I picked up a rat at the first dam set. The rat was caught across the shoulders in the big #4 and nearly cut in two. With a beaver out of the gate set and two squirrels in my marten traps, I felt a little better. Back at camp I wandered down to the lake and there on the shore were the tracks of three timber wolves. They had walked right by since this morning and had stopped to sniff the canoe. They didn't seem too scared of my scent. But then again they had probably never seen or smelt a human before.

As the rest of the day wore down, the wood pile grew along with my frustration. I don't like getting bored. Lobo just stayed out of my way, and at dark I was happy to fix supper, skin the beaver and hit the sack early.

Tomorrow I was going somewhere even if it killed me. And Chain Lakes was my target.

A DAY OF FIRSTS

(November 11)

Heading south along the shore of Hiawatha it was about a mile to
the bottom of the lake. This section of bush with its blow down,
unlevel ground and swamp with Tag Alders so thick you can hardly
move through it taught me a valuable lesson. Patience really is
a virtue! And if I had a little I would not have be standing in
that crap right then. The temperature had actually moved up
during the night, and so my hope of walking on the ice again was
eliminated. The one thought that stayed in my mind as I slogged
my way through this bush was that later on I would get to do it all
over again in reverse. And hopefully I would have a packsack full
of critters.

A mile south and then a mile east to hook up with my trail it
was slow going, made worse by having no traps to check in that
distance. I would have to wait a bit to pull the rat traps along the
river. Finally, however, I arrived at my trailhead and Lobo, I think
was happier than I was. Walking through those thick tags made
me question why God had even put them on this earth. Their only
purpose seemed to be to slap me in the face. That is why on all
my trails, as I walk I am constantly breaking branches and small
trees. Over the course of time it thins out your trail and just makes
walking that much easier.

Nothing was in my mink set but the marten trap on the top of
the hill had a Red squirrel in it, the second a Flying squirrel and

the third a marten caught nicely across the neck and chest. The only problem was that there was nothing left of him but the part between the traps jaws. The wolves had been here and ate my 30 dollar marten plus stole the bait. Resetting with a bit of anger building in me I realized that they had a right to eat also. But could they not go do it somewhere else.

My next set was the beaver bank den set and it held a nice beaver, which I left in the water until the return trip. At the lodge Lobo dashed forward as he will do from time to time and as he rushed around the house all hell broke loose. Snarling, teeth gnashing and yelps followed as I rushed around the lodge. There was Lobo fighting with a wolf that was caught in my mink trap.

My mind does not even have time to register the thought "what is a wolf doing caught in a mink trap" as my gun levels and through the confusion a bullet enters the wolf's brain, ending the probable outcome of Lobo's suicide attempt. Lobo had been in his share of dog fights but this was a wild timber wolf. It was just a small female but it still outweighed him by thirty pounds.

Once I stopped shaking I investigated further as to how a # 1 longspring mink trap had held a 70 pound wolf. I found that caught only by two toes on the back foot the animal had pulled the drown wire out of the water and got her leg all wrapped up in the wire. It looked like it had been there for a few days and had just curled up and slept. I really had to believe that no one had ever caught their first timber wolf with such a pile of bull crap luck.

Sitting down beside this gorgeous animal I checked her teeth, fur and picked her up to guess her weight. That posed another problem. I was already sitting at over a hundred pounds to carry home through that lovely bush. And I was sitting beside another beaver set. Well might as well get it over with. Sure enough I broke the soft ice and there it was another beaver to add to the weight. There was going to be some skinning done in the bush this day for sure.

Covering the wolf with some boughs in case a raven got brave I moved on to my other traps. A marten, two rats and a squirrel were added to my catch. Stopping to check my otter trap I noticed it was sprung. Half expecting another beaver like my last otter trap, I looked down into the water and there staring at me was a face, huge nose, long whiskers and two beady little eyes looking blankly up at me. Thank You! My first otter and within an hour of catching my first wolf. The only thing bad about catching your first of any species is that you can never do it again.

What an amazing day! I was so pumped that I didn't even mind having to make the trip back through that awful bush. Back at the animal stash I started a fire to keep my hands warm while I skinned the beavers. An hour later with my pack bulging from the otter, rats, beaver skins and the other assorted creatures, I hoisted it up on my back and looked at the carcasses. Boy I needed that meat back at home but I was not going to carry it along with all this other stuff. Kicking the boughs that had been on the wolf over the beavers, I hoped that they might still be there on my next trip.

Ok here we go! Grabbing the wolf by a front, and a back leg, I sort of flipped it up and over my head to land on my pack. With the legs on my shoulders pointing to the front, I used them as handles to hold on to. This, while not overly comfortable, seemed to work as I headed out. With what had to be fairly close to my own weight of 140 pounds on my back, I did feel the need to rest every once in awhile. Finding a good log that had fallen down I would lean back on it and rest the pack and wolf right on the log without having to take the pack off. This always seemed easier to me than dropping the pack and then having to lift it up again. As long as the weight is off your shoulders it relieves the stress on you.

Finally arriving at the lake, the sun was starting to set behind the trees right across from where I stood. Oh how I wished the ice had firmed up during the day, but I knew better and with a grunt I carried on, knowing that as bad as the mornings trip had been this would be much worse. Ya right! I was not prepared for the absolute miserable time I would have for the next several hours.

The walking was ok, but the problem was that there was not that much just straight walking. It was all climbing, squeezing through, crawling under or tripping over. As the sun sank further and the light faded, I lost count of how many times I ended up on my face, or on my back as the weight pulled me over. The more tired I got, the easier it was for me to fall. Keeping the lake within sight on my right side, I finally arrived back at camp with cuts, bruises and a particularly sorry attitude.

I was too tired even to cook so with a coffee and a piece of bannock I was asleep in minutes. Even unloading the pack could wait till morning. Mother Nature had seriously kicked my butt today folks.

(November 12)

Well! You know I had said that I was going somewhere yesterday even if it killed me. It was a good try there, but you missed me. It was just a flesh wound. I felt beat up for sure. My legs were stiffer than I ever remembered. This was a grand day to hang around camp and skin my catch. Maybe cut some firewood, if I felt like it later.

But right now a real good breakfast made of my special items, and coffee, lots and lots of coffee. The weather was about the same so the ice conditions were actually a little worse if anything. The wolves had walked along the edge of the ice but for the most part they were lighter than me and they had four feet to spread their weight on compared to my two. I did however slink far enough out on the ice to put a fishing line down with a small Daredevil and a piece of a beavers tongue on it for bait.

With breakfast cooking I took the extra grouse meat and cut it into quarter inch strips; rubbed salt into it and hung it on the wire over the stove pipe to let it dry out. Keeping the can from my Klik for another lamp I noticed that my potato supply was getting a little low also. I had brought only one twenty five pound burlap bag of potatoes and I had known that they would not last long. Probably less than half of them were now left in the bag.

Relaxing with a coffee over my morning meal I had decided to skin the wolf first. Boy when you bring those things in from the cold and add some heat it really brings out the smell. I had read somewhere that they love to roll and rub in anything that they find that smells bad like dead animals or animal scent pads. Probably just to make the trappers who kill them gag. Or it could be to cover their scent, so their prey can't identify them. Lobo was quite cautious with the dead wolf, walking stiff legged around it. It was too tight in the close confines of the camp so I took it outside and hung it from a tree to skin. I was not totally new to this, having skinned a few coyotes down south, but it still took me a good two hours at least to skin and stretch.

Into the cabin went the stretcher with the hide on it. I had to let it partially dry and the flip it fur side out like a giant marten. Bringing the otter out with me I tried to decide; clean skin or rough skin? Otters I knew were like beavers in the fact that the hide is difficult to separate from the skin. You can clean skin them, which is where you leave all the fat and meat on the body, or you rough skin them, where you pull the hide off as fast as you can taking lots of fat and meat with it to be scraped off later. Now I do not like rough skinning beavers so it stands to reason that I wouldn't like rough skinning otters. Makes sense right?

So clean skinning it was. Two hours and several small holes in the hide later I decided that I didn't like clean skinning otters. My next would be done differently. I really don't like putting holes in my furs. The value drops so much and I have to work too hard for them to waste money like that.

My semi-rough skinned beavers got put on the board next. Nailing them at the four corners I scraped the edges and then completely nailed all around, keeping about an inch and a half between the nails. Then I started scraping with a pushing or pulling motion till all the fat and meat was in one piece in the center of the pelt. I scraped it clean off and tossed it to Lobo. This was like candy to him and he begged for more. "Slow down dog, there is one more coming but I'm not that fast". As he sat there some competition showed up.

My Whiskey Jack buddies were back! I took a little piece of scrap and held it up for him. One flew right down and scooped it out of my hand. Finishing my second beaver I occasionally threw the birds some scraps. Giving Lobo the big piece I held one up for the bird and he flew down and landed right on my fingers. That was so darn cool! For the next half an hour I fed them and watched as they took the food and stuck it on some branch or in the crotch of a tree for later use.

Occasionally checking the thermometer I noticed the slow but steady drop in temperature over the course of the day. One degree at a time till it was down to 28 degrees. If this keeps up I might get to the Little Fraser river trail tomorrow. With that in mind I decided to hurry and check the Pody lake trail before dark. Ya I know I said I would relax but my legs had recovered and I wanted to be moving again.

With a couple hours of daylight left I hurried down the trail and by the time I had reached the first beaver trap on the dam I had a marten in my pack. There were tracks all over the dam and they disappeared under the ice. Otters! Now I was excited. Yes the trap was gone! Grabbing the drown wire I pulled and could feel the added weight on the wire. Chopping the ice to make the hole big enough for the animal to make it out, I was hoping to catch my second otter. But it just turned out to be a beaver. I mean right on, a beaver! With three beavers out of this house I really should have pulled the trap but I wanted one of those otters so I left it there for one more checking.

Another marten and a squirrel were added to the pack by the time I reach the house beside Little Pody Lake. With just a half inch of ice holding the pole I shook it loose and gave it a tug. Yes something in there! "Two traps, two beavers" I think to myself as I pulled it from the water. But no, this time it was an otter! They must have come all the way down the small creek under the ice. Cool, two days two otters!

Another great day! But even great days come to an end and this one was running out faster than I expected. Better quit messing around and get home. Rushing to the mink set, I turned around as soon as I could see that it was not sprung. Walking at a good clip, which for me was about four and a half miles per hour, I made it back shortly after the sun had set behind the cloud bank that was moving in.

Over supper, I checked my map and decided that I would make a bit of an alteration to the trail I had just come off of. Where I hit the creek it was about a mile and a half to Little Pody and from there following the lake and then Pody Creek it was at least three and a half miles to Pody Lake. From the first beaver house I could head straight west along the creek to its headwaters and from there overland to Pody Lake. The difference would be four miles of walking compared to six miles. Plus then when the ice was solid enough I would have a nice circle trip. Cause I really hated all this backtracking all the time, it seemed like such a waste of time.

But right now I had some skinning to take care of! With the otter hung up near the back of the cabin to dry, it was at the back because I remembered at the OTA convention someone had been speaking about otter skinning and they had mentioned that too much heat would singg the fur, (singg being when the tips of the fur curl or split) and that would decrease the value by at least fifty percent. Two hours later the skinning was finished except for the otter which was still a little wet. It might have to wait till I got back from the Little Fraser River trail tomorrow, if I was able to get there at all. Mother Nature was not cooperating with me and she had stalled the thermometer at 28 degrees.

Checking the map again over a cup of coffee, I was amazed at the size of Nagagami Lake! It was a huge bowl with a couple fingers sticking out. And below that somewhere (as my map was cut off,) was the train tracks, twenty three miles, according to the game warden in Hearst. Wondering again how Bill and Don were doing on their trap line, I finally fell asleep. I was awakened by the dog as he tried to push his way into the cabin. Opening the door to let him in I was asleep again in seconds. Later that night a whine from Lobo to go outside only elicited a "shut up" from me. Which he listened to, and the rest of the night was uninterrupted.

(November 13)

My eyes snapped open. What was it that awoke me? Another blast of cold air hit my face, coming from the unsealed doorway. Slipping out of bed and into my pants, I flipped the stove draft open and headed outside. With axe in hand as usual I hurried down to the lake. Getting as far as my fishing line without any creaking or cracking it gave me hope. Several steps farther and I took a strong swing of the axe.

Pulling back the axe it slipped out and along with it my hopes of travelling that day. Following the axe head was water bubbling up through the ice. Now I'm not overly nervous about travelling on thin ice but when you can put an axe through with one chop, even I won't travel far on it. There would be another slow day in camp before I was able to travel north again. But plan "B" came into effect then. I was blazing the trail to Pody Lake.

"Big" Pody Lake is four miles long but nowhere is it more than five hundred yards wide. About three quarters of the way up the lake is a creek system that flows in from the east. From the end of that creek there is a spot that is less than a mile to cut across the height of land and join with the headwaters of the Little Fraser River. Now that would be a long but great circle trail, but I would definitely have to build a line camp on Pody Lake somewhere. But the chance of that being done this year was slim to none; I did have to leave something for me to do the next year.

Even though, I was sure I would be coming in early next year to build a proper cabin, I hoped that I would have time to get a second, smaller camp on Pody Lake. Not that I didn't like my dugout cave dwelling, but I'm just not a bear. Getting that trail blazed across and seeing some new territory sounded like a great "plan B' to me. Good! Feeling better now I decided that my wolf hide was dry enough to turn so I would do that before starting my trek. And at least I would still get to check some traps, even if it was only a few, and I had just checked them yesterday.

So, in short order, Lobo and I were on our way. In my pocket I dropped some of the grouse jerky that I had made the night before. It had not turned out to bad if maybe a little salty. I decided to try some with the next beaver that I caught that was reasonably fresh. Leaving the gun at camp, because it was a pain trying to blaze a trail with just one hand, we started out. As we moved down the trail it seemed like I was having déjà-vu. As we moved down the trail it seemed like I was having déjà-vu. Didn't I just say that? I had been here recently! Oh yes, it was yesterday. But I would not be on the same trail for long.

Arriving at the first beaver house I turned right this time and followed the tiny creek for a half mile to its source, which ended up being a pond, lined with floating bog and Black Spruce trees. Not a piece of beaver food as far as the eye could see. And of course no beavers either which was just slightly disappointing so I continued west, keeping an eye out for a small pond off to the left that needed to be checked out. I must have missed it to the north so blazing a tree at the point where I thought should be the closest point to the pond, I carried on, turning slightly to the north.

After two hours of compassing and blazing I broke out on the shore of one of the prettiest lakes you can imagine. Heavily wooded for the most part with snow covered rocky points and a myriad of little islands, it was truly a postcard type setting. Funny though, I had hit the lake at a spot about a mile north of my intended arrival point. I guess I had not been paying close enough attention to my compassing. Sometimes I did that while blazing a trail. I had a tendency to always wander to my right, so I had better keep track of that if I ever had any real long trails to blaze. Maybe I should have just compassed and blazed on the return trip. Turning back I watched for sign until I reached the spot where I had left the mark to go look for that pond. There I turned straight south and within a couple hundred yards I spotted the opening off to my left.

The pond was dead, but it looked like the beavers had been here maybe two or three years ago. Oh well, better luck on the next pond I hoped. Back at the spot where we had left our trail four hours earlier I decide that I would run down and check the traps to Little Pody Lake. One sprung beaver trap and a Red squirrel were all the reward that I got. But at least that beaver trap was reset and ready to catch something.

Walking back I noticed that the temperature was dropping as the cloud bank was being pushed back to the south east. And that was good news to me because with clear skies usually comes colder temperatures. Tomorrow was the day; I could feel it in my bones. Fixing myself a good supper I did some chores around the camp and brushed out my fur. Being bored again I decided on an early night; for an early start in the morning.

In the middle of the night my eyes snapped open. What the heck had woke me? There it was again! A screeching, moaning noise that sounded almost, painful! What was that? Throwing on my boots and coat I crawled outside and listened. Gosh but the temperature had dropped, the thermometer read minus five. There! It was coming from the lake. The ice was cracking and the sounds were so eerie; a wailing that reverberated across the lake like it was coming from a living thing. Back to bed for the duration as the ice song serenaded me back to sleep, that's it! It almost sounded like whales singing.

THE DANGERS OF IMPATIENCE

(November 14)

My eyes opened and I was moving before they even focused properly. Throwing on my clothes I ran down the hill to the now solidly frozen lake. But what the heck, the lake was criss-crossed with black lines that were about five feet wide. They ran from shore to shore, or from shore to join with another line, or from line to line. The entire lake looked like a giant jigsaw puzzle! One of the lines started at the rock point just to the left of me so I walked over to check it out. The white ice was cracking under my weight. How could that be at minus 15 degrees?

I scurried over to the black ice road and there I could see what had happened. The ice cracked over night which was the sounds that I had heard and the water had seeped up through the crack and flooded a few feet on each side of the crack. This had then produced clear black ice and made little roads that were quite solid all over the lake. It took two or three good swipes to get through the ice and that meant it was safe for me to walk on.

Yes! I was heading north. Since I was on the ice already I decided to run across the lake and check my two sets on the point. The road I was on led straight to the point about fifty yards from my mink set. Checking the ice regularly I made it to the traps and was rewarded with a medium sized marten. The mink trap was frozen into the ice and there were wolf tracks everywhere. They had stolen the bait, collapsed the cubby and generally made a mess of things.

Rebuilding the cubby, I decided to bring a Conibear and some bait back for this set on the way north. I had just about given up hope for today when the white ice was cracking under my weight, but now I was excited to get on the move. Looking north through the narrows I could see that the ice roads zig-zagged across the lake for as far as I could see. It would mean a little extra walking having to follow these trails but with the trip only being about eight miles it would not make that much of a difference. Back to the cabin I hurried where I made a quick breakfast and coffee. Packing my gear, traps, wire, bait, pliers and axe I headed out.

These ice roads were very slippery so I moved mainly by sliding my feet, not really lifting them at all; you keep better control if your feet never leave the ice. And with the weight of this pack (probably 70 pounds with all the traps and bait I had) I didn't want to end up on my butt. This trip was without my gun because of the weight but I really wished I had it. I had a feeling that the animals would be moving in this cold weather.

From one ice trail to another I made my way up the lake until I was getting close to my first beaver set. Here one of the trails led to shore about one hundred yards past the creek, so I took that one. From there I could walk the shoreline to hit my trail. At the point that I was about seventy five yards from the shore my heart sank as I took a step and my foot seemed to sink into the ice. I had felt this feeling before and it never ended well. I could not stop my next step and as my foot hit, I tried to throw myself flat on the ice. It didn't work! My feet were already through and I could feel the ice slowly crumbling under me. I was up to my waist when the movement stopped. Bent over the ice, holding on only by friction, too scared to move I finally realized that I couldn't stay like this for long, so trying to move my weight forward I felt the ice crack again.

This time it was real bad though! The ice had cracked in front of me and now the chunk that I was holding onto was loose. Grabbing the edge of it I held on and was helpless as the weight of my pack and myself slowly tipped the ice over until it hit a point where it just flipped, sending me into and under the water. Funny though, I don't even remember it being cold. All I thought about as the pack pulled me down through the water, until I was laying on the bottom of the lake, was how was I going to get back through that hole in the ice. Struggling out of my pack straps I kicked off the bottom and broke the surface, pushing the ice out of the way.

Lobo was frantic! I clawed my way to the edge closest to the direction I had come from and tried to pull myself up. The ice broke again. Oh boy! I could not keep doing this forever, even though the whole process had not gone on for more than a minute or two so far. But I could sure feel the water now! Calling Lobo over to me he belly crawled close enough that I could get a hold of him. Turning him around it was like he knew what I needed him to do. He dug his claws in and by holding onto his fur I was able to inch my way out onto the ice. I squirmed all the way up until I was fifty feet from the hole and then sat up. I was shaking so bad from the adrenaline that I couldn't stand for a few minutes. Soon however I knew I would need to get moving or I would have other problems to deal with, so with that thought I got up and as fast as possible, headed south.

Funny though, the thing that I remember to this day so vividly is that the wind froze the outside of my clothes to a sheet of ice and the inside layer warmed right up after I got moving; right to the point that when I had returned to camp I was no longer even cold. It was the strangest thing! But then the adrenaline from what had just almost happened got to me and I started shaking like a leaf in a cool autumn breeze. But I had learned a good lesson, you can't rush Mother Nature. The words to my friends in White River came back to me, "Hey it's just the bush, what could go wrong." I guess I had forgotten about the lake.

Stripping down, I put on dry clothes and hung the wet things up to dry. With a hot coffee in hand all was again well in the world.

Except for one thing, I had just lost most of the traps that I had left, one of my axes and the only real packsack that I had with me. I did have a little tiny day pack that held my spare clothes, but it would not even hold one beaver. Thank god I had left my gun at the camp.

Reflecting on the day, I remembered falling through the ice down south which had never been a big deal. I would keep going and if I got to cold just stop and build a fire. But lying on my back on the bottom of the lake struggling to get the pack off my back was a different sort of fun. Two weeks I had been in here, and that's all the time it had taken me to get into trouble. Better be careful buddy! Nothing to do now but relax so I went for a nap, waking in a sweat because I had left the stove going wide open. It must have been 80 degrees in the cabin.

With the temperature the way it was the ice would have to be safe by tomorrow, but you know maybe I'd give it another day to be sure. I decided to take a walk along the shore to the Chain Lakes trail. Ya, and I would stay close to the shore. Since there was some daylight left I figured that I may as well cut some firewood to kill the day. Behind the camp were a lot of scattered White birch trees. They were green but they made a good wood for mixing in with the dry spruce and Jack pine. Cutting one down, I hauled it back to camp, bucked it up and added it to my woodpile.

In my trap behind the camp was a cute little Short Tailed weasel, or ermine as they are called in the winter once their fur turns snow white. I had seen their tracks but back home I had used the big wooden platform rat traps to catch them, but those had all been left down south and it was just a fluke that it had gotten into my marten set. I remembered the book Traplines North and that the ermine were a major part of the boys catch for the winter. Luckily I was not depending on those little guys to make a living. Down south though the weasels that I usually caught were the Long Tailed weasels and they were about twice the size of these little fellows. There is another subspecies also, called the Least weasel and as the name implies it is the smallest of the three. I had never seen one that I could recall though.

Getting close to supper time I went to check my fishing line, hoping for a fresh fish to eat. Pulling it up I noticed the slice of beaver tongue bait was gone. Looking at the hook I had a brain storm and I hurried back up the hill to check on something. Grabbing the small tackle box that I had brought with me I searched and there it was a big heavy spoon with a large treble hook on it. Yes! I was going to try and hook my pack from the bottom of the lake!

However I would still wait till the next day to give the ice time to firm up. With a little more excitement in me now I crawled into the cabin to start supper. My last can of chili and close to the last of my potatoes were on the menu for tonight. Boy with six weeks left before I was getting picked up my food was disappearing faster than I liked. With tomorrows plans all laid out I hit the sack, listened to some radio and jotted down a few notes in my journal. Thinking about how close today had come to being my last I was just glad this didn't happen yesterday. Since it was the thirteenth yesterday maybe I would not have been as lucky as I was today!

Who knows, I was just glad it worked out the way it did. Thanks to Lobo's help.

(November 15)

Up early I broke into my supply of oatmeal for breakfast. I didn't particularly like the stuff but it is cheap and filling so with a hot coffee and a little sugar sprinkled on, it did me fine. With a couple traps and a mitt full of snares stuffed into my tiny packsack I added as much bait as I could fit in there and headed out. Moving south along the shore where I knew the water was shallow I got no sound from the ice at all. That was good news but I still stayed within a few yards of the shore, only moving out to get around a fallen tree here and there.

In no time at all I was at the trail head to the Chain Lakes. My plan was to go south on Lake #3 and check out Lake # 2 and # 1. Climbing the hill that marked the start of my trail I was met by a Red squirrel, man was there no end to those things? My next two sets however, produce two nice marten, one that was almost black. So dark that I thought it was a small fisher when I first saw it. I had never seen an animal that could vary so widely in color from one animal to the next. Even on one animal the color can change dramatically from the head to near the tail.

Lake 3 was solid when I got there so I turned right and pushed my way to Lake 1 where I spotted a nice big beaver house on the far shore. I would come back there to set it after I checked out # 2. It was actually just off to the east of #1 and the creek from it flowed into one arm of # 1 which was shaped like a horse shoe. Cool, # 2 had a live house on it also. I could see why they both had live houses since there were Poplar trees all around both lakes. Heading into the bush I found a nice young Poplar tree about 3 inches thick and cut it down for bait.

On the shore I cut a nice solid dry pole about ten feet long and with the bait pole headed for the lodge. Remembering that once bitten twice shy rule I was very careful around the house. Particularly in close! Where the beavers move in and out of their tunnels the air bubbles that are expelled build up under the ice and prevent freezing. While it is a great way to find the entrances it can also give you a wet foot if you are not careful. So advancing closer and testing with the axe I got to the edge of the feed pile and made my cut, a hole about three feet by one foot. Beautiful clear water is in this lake and on my knees I gazed down into the opening. I could see tiny peeled sticks on the bottom and floating under the edge of the ice. Perfect!

Taking six snares, I wired two snares on opposite sides of the dry pole and then two more right under them and again below those ones. The snares should overlap each other by an inch or so. Then I cut a piece of the bait pole about thirty inches long and it should be two inches or a little less in thickness. Nailing the first one on one side of the dry pole level with the snares I then flipped the set over and nailed another piece on the opposite side. The beaver snares, which are about a ten inch circle cover the length of the bait and as a beaver comes to try and take the poplar he gets tangled up in the snares and quickly expires.

This is a very good set and easy to make, if not time consuming, and the snares are a lot lighter to carry around than the big # 330 Conibears. The next step was to make sure the loose ice was all out of the hole and then you lower the set carefully down into the water and gently push the pole into the bottom. Your last step is to wire a cross pole for safety. This is in case a beaver gets caught before the ice locks the set in place and it will stop him from dragging the whole deal under the ice.

On the way back to Lake 1, I put a marten cubby between the two lakes, and taking an extra piece of bait with me, I aimed for the house on # 1. Cutting a good dry pole on the way I made another set just like the last one. Once finished I went to the house to check the chimney and I noticed a spruce tree behind the house that looked weird. The top looked like it had been cut off and there was a large pile of snow on the top. Not sure why it even caught my attention but something was hanging from the snow. That's weird, it looked like a chain. I knocked the snow away and sure enough, it was a chain. Actually it was six of them. There were six #330 Conibears piled on the top of this tree! What the? Someone in the past must have been trapping here and then forgot them or left them on purpose with the intent of coming back. If that was the case then they were poaching and either way these were mine now. Cool, I had more traps to set. And since this house had what looked like a well defined entrance I eased over close to the house and gave the ice a smack. Sure enough the ice was less than an inch thick. Air bubbles blasted up and there were a lot of peeled sticks floating under the ice. All signs of a very well used tunnel.

Finding two nice dry poles on shore I cut them off about eight feet long and made my entrance set with one of my new traps. Heading north again I added a marten set in the bush between Lake 1 and 3. Back at Lake 3, I found a stick in the bank den set. He must have been going to eat and the stick got there ahead of the beaver. Lucky for him I guess. The entrance set held a medium sized beaver which I left in the water till the return trip.

Picking up another squirrel and a mink on the way to check my otter trap, I noticed, from a short distance, that the trap was sprung. I could see no otter tracks so I was half expecting another beaver but it was not even that good. Just a rat! Carrying two of the 330's that I had found, I moved up through the system past where I had seen the huge bull moose and into new territory. No one home today but the tracks told me that they had been here recently. Looked like a real big one and a cow calf pair. Covering the ¾ of a mile of grass land in no time, I arrived at Lake 7.

The creek mouth had a beaver dam with a five foot wide hole torn through it. If there were any beavers here they would have fixed the dam. This was an actual lake though, with what looked like deep water even without the beaver dam. Seven and eight were really just one lake divided by a big beaver dam. Below the dam I saw otter tracks and a spot where there was blood and fish scales on the snow. That got me to wondering what kind of fish would be in these tiny lakes. Probably just suckers but I guessed there could also be pike.

From the dam I could see a huge house across the pond. The house had another nice entrance, and along with that set, I cut a dry pole and a small poplar tree that I had to go into the bush quite a ways to find. Cutting a piece of the poplar about 18 inches long with a branch about 6 inches from the top, I took the dry pole and checked the water depth at the hole I had cut for this set. Nailing the bait stick about three feet from the bottom with the branch at the top end, I then squeezed the 330 on to the bait stick so that the branch went into the springs. The trigger was placed right by the bottom of the branch since this was where the beavers would come and try to chew the branch off. Wiring the trap chain to the dry pole, it got lowered into the water and anchored like a snare set. Fast and effective, that's how I like my sets.

Checking the suns location I estimated that it was about time to head home. Lake 9 was calling me but I ignored her. With no traps left to set it would have just be an exploration trip and I just didn't have time right now. So, pointing myself to the south I got under way. Picking up my fur as I traveled, replacing traps where the animals were too frozen to get the trap off, I arrived at the beaver. These traps were pulled and the beaver was hooked on to my tow rope. It was about ten feet long and has a three inch loop on one end and a three foot loop on the other.

Taking a five inch spike that I carried in my pocket with the rope, I stuck the nail through the cartilage between the beaver's nostrils. The small loop went over the nail and the big loop over my shoulders. This was a very easy way to move beavers and I have pulled as many as three in a row like this. I also carried a shorter rope for Lobo to pull if my load gets too big. You just have to be very careful that there is enough snow on the ground or the fur will be damaged as you pull it over sticks and such. It is easier dragging on a snowshoe trail rather than this boot trail as the animal has a tendency to flop from one boot hole to the other instead of sliding along. But it was still easier than trying to get that beaver in that little pack.

Arriving at Hiawatha Lake with the sun just touching the western horizon Lobo and I skirted the lake shore and were safely back at camp in no time, with bait, and dog food to boot! More important was the fact that we had found some more houses to set. Inside the animals were hung up to dry, and some coffee water was heated up. Too early for supper so I cared for my furs that were already dried, cleaning any grease off the hide and brushing the fur free of dirt, blood or anything that doesn't belong there.

With the animals still not ready for skinning I tackled supper. Wait a second, I ran down to check my fish lines. Yes! Fresh fish for supper tonight, and walleye at that! My first of the year! So there really were walleye in this lake. It sure made a tasty meal along with some bannock and jam. Relaxing with a full belly and a hot coffee in hand, it made a guy wonder what a difference a day makes. Sitting here all warm and toasty when a little more than 24 hours ago I was sitting at the bottom of a frozen lake. What a wacky world. I wondered to myself, what were all the poor people doing right at that moment?

Tomorrow my plan was to head up the lake and try to retrieve my packsack. Not too sure how long it might take or even if I would find it, I made plans to check the Pody Lake trails after returning and then off to Ahmabel Lake the next day. With the beaver still wet and the rest still frozen I decided to skin them all tomorrow and made an early night of it. Falling asleep to the sounds of Kapaskasing radio, I awoke at some point to turn it off and then lights out.

PACKSACK RESCUE

(November 16)

Daylight caught me fed and with everything skinned other than the beaver; it could wait till I got back from the north end of the lake. The north wind was howling straight down the length of Hiawatha Lake but with only two miles to travel I hardly even noticed it before I was standing over what used to be a hole in the ice. Cutting a big hole right above where my best guess of where the pack would be, I lowered the big hook, which was now tied to a rope down into the water. Letting it hit the bottom I dragged it as far as the hole would allow and snagged nothing but some stiff weedy plants.

Ok, so I was going to need a really big hole. Chopping for awhile I tried again and again. No luck! Back to chopping and soon the hole was bigger than the one I fell through. Hours went by and the biggest thing I brought up was a piece of driftwood. Then my brain kicked in and I headed to shore to cut a pole that was at least twelve feet long. Back at the hole I used the pole to poke at the bottom of the lake and look for something that felt like a lump. Within minutes I felt what could be the pack. It was solid feeling but not hard like a rock.

Marking the spot I took the lure and tried to snag it. No luck again. After another half an hour I headed back to shore and cut a pole that had a strong branch near the bottom. Cutting the branch off at about six inches I used it to try and snag the pack straps. On my third attempt I hooked on the something heavy. Pulling carefully, I was finally rewarded at the sight of my pack breaking the surface. Grabbing the strap before it could slip back into the water I heaved it out onto the ice and sat back relieved. Honest to God, you would have thought I had just won the lottery, I was so happy! Leaving the traps, bait and wire there to be picked up in the morning, I took the food and the pack to dry it out over the stove.

Now the big question; did I have enough time to go and check the Pody Lake traps? Ya I did! On a rush though, I hurried out and stopped quick to check the point traps. The wolves, looked like two of them, had again stolen the bait from the mink set. Oh those things were getting annoying. I would rebait on the way out tomorrow but I really needed to get a move on.

Lobo seemed comfortable at camp so I told him to stay, and with a hot coffee and a few bites of bannock I took off down the trail. With two marten and the same amount of squirrels, I returned home about an hour after dark. There just did not seem to be enough time in a day out here. And I knew that it would only get worse as we got closer to Christmas. My fur catch was starting to pile up nicely and suddenly I could not estimate what I had caught. Taking a minute to get an accurate count it ended up being eleven beaver, fourteen marten, seven mink, ten rats, two otters, twelve squirrels, one wolf and a weasel. Not a record catch, but I was happy with it considering the amount of work that had to get finished when I had arrived.

Tomorrow was again going to be a big day. I trimmed down my load, leaving the food and bringing extra traps instead. The food that was at the camp on Ahmabel would have to do for the first trip. For now, with my nightly chores finished, I sipped on a last cup of Java and let the radio lull me to sleep. Tomorrow I was seeing new country again. I couldn't wait!

ARE YOU KIDDING ME!

(November 17)

Finally, I was again on my way to Ahmabel Lake. While I was enjoying my breakfast of oatmeal with bannock and honey, I dished out a helping of dog food for Lobo in case I used all the bait making mink and marten sets. My pack had ninety percent dried out over night, so with my gear loaded and my fur as mouse proofed as it could be, I stepped out onto the trail. Hurrying across the narrows to throw a chunk of bait in my mink set, I then turned north up the lake and found a marten in my other mink set. Cool but do I take it with me or leave it? There was no way I was leaving it on the ground for the mice to find so I decided to hang it in a tree with a piece of wire.

With another nice big male in the middle trap between the lake and the Little Fraser River, I exchanged that trap and hung the filled one from a branch. Once at the river I bypassed the two beaver traps to the west as I would check them on the return trip. Pulling all my rat and mink drown wire sets, I did catch three muskrats and one mink, I noticed a weird looking lump on the top of a dead broken off tree so I watched it as I got closer. Close enough I guessed, as the huge bird took wing and floated effortlessly over the grassy meadow. I had never seen a Great Gray Owl before but I knew them from books and this was a beauty. Obviously looking for a meal and I wondered to myself if they were one of the reasons I had not seen even a single marten track out in the open grassy areas. Would they eat marten? I didn't see why not.

He drifted to the far side of the opening and I moved past him to get to my beaver traps. Picking more sets up on the way, I added another rat and a marten to the bag. The beaver sets were frozen in with one having a huge beaver in it. The animals back was sticking out of the ice a little bit and the birds had been picking at it. The damage was not that bad but it would degrade the value for sure. But these traps were pulled now since that was two beavers from this house. On the dam there were otter tracks that disappeared down and under the ice below the dam.

Just past the pond, there was another of the huge owls. The mate of the first one, possibly? Do they mate for life like eagles and Canada geese I wondered? All I knew for sure was that they were cool to watch with their big, round, faces turning to watch me as I walked past them.

Cutting through the bush in places where the river closed in, I would notice marten tracks but out in the open it would be only mink or otter. The odd fox track was around as well and I should make some sets but just didn't seem to have the time. As I got closer to Otter Lake I started looking for places to set wolf snares. At one spot I blocked the trail with guide sticks to try and guide the wolves into my snare, and a short distance further in a patch of thick tag alders I placed another snare for them. Liking the set, I kept going and finally arrived at the lake.

At third Otter Lake I put in two quick sets, having already been there I knew what sets I was going to make, so I cut the needed poles on the way. One entrance and a bait snare set were the ticket here. When I got to the river exit out of Otter Lake I noticed that the river really was a river now. A lot more water flowing, with many small ponds joined by rapids made sure that for the next mile, there was no chance of using a canoe in the future years if I ever got the notion.

In the second pond I found another live house so I threw in a snare bait set between the feed bed and the dam. Downriver a ways, I crossed to the north side of the river to get away from some rocky cliffs and as my trail was running between the river and a steep hill I came across a fallen tree. This thing must have been four or five feet wide at the base and a good three feet wide where I crawled over. From the fallen tree I left the creek and headed straight east. The river had taken a turn to the south so I blazed a trail down the gentle slope, and after a short two hundred yards, Ahmabel Lake opened up to me.

Not sure where the cabin was located I had two options. I was about one third of the way up the lake from the south shore. That gave me a two out of three chance that the cabin was to the north. So that was the way I went. North up the western shore and in less than a mile I had spotted the camp on a small point sticking out into the lake. The lonely plywood structure stood out as the only sign of man that I had seen for some time.

Standing beside the snow covered dock I looked down at Lobo. He seemed to be thinking the same thing I was, "It ain't a mansion, but it is still nicer than our hole in the ground".

Climbing the slight rise from the shore, I noticed a lump in the snow that turned out to be two boats flipped over and leaning, one on the other. The weathered plywood over frame construct has a small deck attached and a couple windows on the east and south walls. A stove pipe sticking through the tar paper covered roof assured me that at least I would have heat this night. A small shed and an outhouse were the only other buildings on this site. Checking the shed I found nothing but a bucksaw and some tin cans with nails in them. Moving on to the cabin itself, (I didn't feel the need to check the outhouse) I tried the door and thankfully it was not locked. I have since learned that most camps in the wilderness are left unlocked on the off chance that someone might need to make use of them in an emergency. Besides, locks only keep honest people out. Once inside I saw two rows of bunk beds along the north and west walls with a mattress for each bed leaning against the wall. Not a blanket in sight. But why would there be? If they were left here the mice would destroy them. Well this was a pickle.

My first order of business was to check on my food supply. It didn't take me long to take stock of what was here. A quarter of a jar of jam and even less of peanut butter with a box that was half full of pancake mix. A tiny jar of instant coffee and a little sugar rounded out my supply. Well thank god for the coffee! That was the food supply that the game warden had said should be here. Oh well, better than nothing I guess, beggars can't be choosers. But it didn't look like I would be here for two nights now. With some daylight left I decide to explore the rest of the lake and see what's up with the beavers. Now I wished I had brought my gun. I already could have shot at least one grouse today.

On the west shore right around the point from the cabin I found a nice lodge. Looking up toward the north end of the lake I saw a black dot on the ice by the river mouth. Moving closer I looked again and it was gone. There it was again and gone. An otter was catching food and eating it on the ice. The river mouth was wide open and there were a lot of tracks all over the snow. This was where the Fraser River started to build in size as it flowed north to join with the Kenogami, and eventually the Albany Rivers.

The day was winding down and I needed to get to the cabin and eat some supper. I would explore a little ways upstream, towards East Ahmabel in the morning. It was, according to the map, less than two miles to the lake and I would be able to cover that and be back in an hour or two. At least I would know how many beaver traps I needed to bring on the next trip. Twenty minutes later I was in camp and getting the pancake mix ready. Pouring half the box into a bowl I... what the heck! Picking the little brown pellets out of the pancake mix I could not believe my luck. Mouse terds!

There were mouse terds in my supper! Well I was not going to go hungry so I picked them all out and flung them into the stove. They wouldn't kill me, I hoped!

Cooking up a half dozen flapjacks I threw two to the dog and the rest I spread a little PB and J on them. With a hot coffee it made a filling meal. As long as I didn't think of the mouse crap that I was sure I could taste, that is. Looking at the bed situation I decide to try sleeping on a mattress and use another one as a blanket. With a good fire going all night it should keep me warm enough. I would have to be getting up every couple of hours to add firewood but if that's what it took then I guess that's what I was going to do.

With a coffee in hand I stood on the porch, the cold breeze hitting me in the face. Looking out over the moon lit lake I just imagined that this was what the trappers that first came to this land must have felt. A calming almost tranquil feeling as you listen to the silence, broken occasionally by the cracking of a tree freezing or the ice moaning, but mainly just pure and complete silence. And there, to add to the moment, off from the south came the sorrowful howl of Timber wolves. How can this moment get any better! Listening for a few minutes they fell silent. I headed back inside, a smile of contentment on my face. What a night!

(November 18)

On the eastern horizon the light was just starting to turn the sky a light shade of pink. I slid from between the mattresses and filled the stove before jumping back into bed to wait for the cabin to warm up. Ten minutes later I was ready for a hot cup of coffee. How a night that started so amazing could end up being so uncomfortable is beyond me. I would wake up from the shivering, fill the stove and eventually fall back asleep. Only to be jolted awake again as the cold crept into my back. At some point during the night I had pulled the bed right up beside the stove and would roll over and over. Toasting the front then the back, needless to say it was not my best night's sleep. So dawn was a welcome to me and I could not wait to get on the trail. I decided to go and check out the river first and then eat before I headed back, so with my second coffee inside me I moved out, with Lobo in tow.

Once out on the lake I noticed a dark cloud bank moving in from the west. Any serious accumulation of snow and I would have to break out my snowshoes. Straight east of the cabin, flowing in from East Ahmabel Lake, was the river that I was heading for. There was about two hundred yards of bush before the creek opened up into wide grassy meadows that were flooded by the beavers. The river here was more like a two mile long and a hundred foot wide beaver pond. No real current because of the dam holding back all the water and I could walk right up the middle of the river without worry of weak ice.

By the time I reached the wide open marsh surrounding the lake I had found two beaver houses. Turning back happy, I planned on setting them on my next trip to this area. Building a marten pole set just before the lake, I made it back to camp and got my breakfast under way. Pouring the rest of my pancake mix into the bowl for mixing, I just stared as the last bit fell out. Lucky I had a strong stomach because there in the bowl was a dead, dried up mouse that had been in the bottom of the box. Great, some meat with my pancakes! I usually prefer sausages but I guess this would have to do. Pinching its tail between my fingers I gave it a toss and picked the rest of the terds out, added some water and dove in. If it hadn't made me sick yet, I didn't think it was going to.

Throwing a couple of the flapjacks to Lobo again he wolfed them down, as did I. If a dead mouse's terds are the worst thing I eat in my life I would be doing ok I think. Finally fed, watered and packed up we moved on down the trail, making a mink/marten set along the west shore of the lake. Turning west on my trail, I covered ground rapidly, setting a marten trap here and a mink trap there. Nothing was in my first beaver set so I moved on to Otter Lake and past. At third Otter I had a nice beaver in the entrance set. Now with beaver in tow I added a weasel from a mink set and a squirrel from a marten set and picked up the beaver from the day before.

Getting to where the trail turned off to Hiawatha, I dropped my load of animals and headed to the beaver sets west of the trail. With a muskrat in the dam set and a beaver in the bank den set I threw the beaver over my shoulder and I trudged back to the pack and hooked up all three beaver in tandem. Using wire from the back legs to the nail through the nose of each beaver, they dragged fairly well through the bush. With a marten in the last trap before the lake, I noticed as I was removing the animal, that the snow had started. And quite heavy I might add!

This added a new dimension to the trip. The ice roads that I had followed were not visible anymore with this fresh snow but I didn't think I had to worry about the ice safety. But, with an inch of snow on those slick trails it made for delicate walking. With the drag from the beavers, even though it was minimal, I almost went for a spill several times as I would suddenly hit super slippery ice. I carried on gingerly and just as I was about to enter the narrows I look off to my right and there stood three moose, a cow and twin calves, staring at me from not fifty yards away. Maybe they had never seen a person dragging three beavers behind him before. Or just never seen a person period!

Finally back at camp, I crawled in dragging my catch behind me. The first thing I noticed was that I had sprung a leak in the cabin roof. There was an icicle hanging from the ridge pole and a bit of a stalactite growing from the ground. Oh well it would melt once I got the fire going, which I did right away. Hanging the animals, I put the coffee water on and sorted out my gear. Now a good meal free of mouse crap and I took a moment to relax. Soon enough I headed outside and checked the camp set, reset the trap, and threw away the flying squirrel tail. The snow has covered any sign of what ate it, so with axe in hand, I checked my fishing lines and brought a pail of water back with me.

With my day finished I laid back on my bed, listening to some music and jotting down the last two days happenings. A whine at the door and I opened it to let Lobo in but he just stood there looking at me. In or out dog, make a decision. "Ok, I'll make it for you", and the door got shut. Kicking back I wondered again how the guys were doing on their line so far. They should be in full swing. I wished for some lynx here like I knew that they had. But they had rabbits down there. Not like here where a lynx would have a hard time finding a meal. Falling asleep with visions of lynx traps full of the gorgeous creatures, I didn't move again till the morning sun was clear of the trees.

A BATTLE WITH THE WOLVES

(November 19)

Too soon, as I lay in bed enjoying the calm, came the morning. Chain Lakes awaited me and I tried to guestimate what my catch would be for the day. Breakfast and coffee over with, I readied another drag rope. This one however was for Lobo, and was a little shorter than the one I used. With my pack all loaded up I slid my boots into my snowshoe harnesses and threw the pack on my back.

The night had left me another five inches of snow and it would be a treat to make my way from now on with the shuffling gait of the snowshoe traveler. If you have never walked in snowshoes it seems awkward at first. Most people try and lift the shoe instead of just lifting your foot, pointing your toe to the ground and sliding the snowshoe along the snows surface. If the shoe comes up with your heel then your harness is not set properly. I use nothing but the Bates harness as it is designed to come off if you fall through the ice (not that that could ever happen), with just a turn of your foot. The only adjustment I had made was to take a two inch nail and hammer it into the rubber heel of my boots. When I was not snowshoeing I pushed it all the way in but when I strapped on the shoes I pulled it out a half an inch or so. Like I said, I like my harnesses very loose and this stopped the heel strap from falling off.

Starting off breaking trail would be a little harder on Lobo because the trail was soft for a bit but it should be firmed up by the time we headed home this evening. Stepping out, I reran through my plans for today as I traveled. Break the trail all the way to Lake 9, set some wolf snares, hopefully set a beaver house on #9 and catch a pile of fur. Wondering if I had an animal at the point sets I looked that way and there to my amazement were two wolves standing on the ice, staring toward the mink set.

Now what! I was a hundred yards from shore, and my rifle! If I went back they might be gone by the time I returned, but I had to try! Hurrying, I dropped the pack and did the odd looking snowshoe run back to camp. Kicking off the shoes I rushed into the camp and darn it, I couldn't find the bullets for my 30.06! Where did I put those things? Finally locating them I hurried back and yes I was right. They were gone! Oh well I would have felt really stupid if I had kept going and never even tried. Still, really cool to see them and Lobo, the ever vigilant dog that he was, had never even known that they were there.

Once at the mink set, you guessed it. The trap was sprung and the bait gone. Sooner or later these wolves would get their reward for stealing my bait all the time. The marten trap was empty also so I moved on down the lake. Gosh it felt great to be travelling in the snowshoes again. The easy gait ate up the distance and was much easier on me than slogging through the snow with just my boots on.

I made it to Lake 3 with not a piece of fur in my marten traps so I pointed my shoes to the south and Lake 1 and 2. Hey Dave! How about a nice mink between 3 and 1? Sure don't mind if I do. And it was a real nice dark male! Turning, I caught a marten in my cubby set between 1 and 2, and a beaver in the snare set. Replacing the snare and two others that the beaver had totally destroyed, I also needed to replace the bait since the other beavers ate it all. Every bit of the bait was gone, other than an inch around each nail head. Retracing my steps to Lake 1, I added another beaver from the entrance set.

Now I could start to worry about the load I was going to end up with. But a good worry, as you can only hope for those days when you catch too much fur. With a sprung trap at my marten set, I continued on past the lakes and upon reaching Lake 8, I had caught just two squirrels and a Whiskey Jack in my traps. That's weird and I hoped it wasn't my buddy from camp. But I knew it wasn't, those guys were all over this land, them and their screeching cousins the Blue Jay. And since the snow had arrived, with it came my little friends the Black Capped Chickadees. Many a lonely day in the bush was brightened with a flock of these little guys following along with me as I traveled, always singing their song. Chicadee-dee-dee, chickadee-dee-dee. They were so neat to have around.

Again just below the dam, between 7 and 8 there was otter sign where they had been eating fish. That started to formulate a plan in my head, and that was always trouble for something. Setting a mink trap at the bottom of the dam I climbed over it and crossed to the house. My snare set produced another big beaver but the 330 was not touched. Remembering to cut some spruce boughs to cover the hole with I then, using a snowshoe as a shovel, piled as much snow on top as I could. That should help slow down the ice from forming and make it easier to check next time.

Moving back into new country again got my imagination going. Throwing a marten set in between Lake 8 and 9, I found Lake 9 was a long narrow lake with sheer rock shores and nothing but Spruce lining the edge of the lake. From the looks of it I didn't expect to find a live house, and I had no surprises in that respect. At the end of the lake I remembered that it was only about a mile from here to the Little Fraser River and my trail. Trying to decide if I should just blaze the trail or set the two marten traps I had with me. Just blazing won out and I covered the ground quickly, following a drainage that took me right to the river. Making a few large blazes so I would notice them if I was coming from the other way, I turned and headed back.

It was getting late as I picked up my fur and with my beaver in tow I arrived at Lake 3. I hooked up the other beavers, one more on my tow line and one in my pack. Taking our time we wound our way through the thick stand of Spruce, and into the more open area of Poplar and Jack Pine trees. About a quarter mile or so from the lake shore the bush thickened right up again, with the thick stand of small Black Spruce trees that I could barely get through with this heavy pack. But finally the trail dropped off at the big hill that announced the presence of the lake.

Half sliding on the shoes and half walking I almost took a nose dive into the snow when the beavers slid right down on to the backs of my snowshoes. That was fun but enough playing around. I really hoped to have something on my fishing lines because a feed of fresh fish would have done wonders for me that night. There were fresh fox tracks all along the shore line and at one spot, where the brush was very thick, I made three trails from the shore into one spot and hung a chunk of bait in a tree. On each of the trails I placed a fox snare knowing that they would follow my snowshoe trail for the easy meal. This was a very simple set that I had great success with down south. It would probably work better once the snow got even deeper.

Loading back up I moved out and was on the main part of the lake when I came across a single wolf track. This was by far the biggest track I had seen since I had landed and setting my hand inside the track, it was actually bigger than my hand was. He had travelled north to south on the ice, and as I back tracked him, he looked like he was coming right from my mink set. He had stopped about fifty feet out from the set and milled around somewhat, never going to close to the trap. Following my trail back I found where he had crossed it. The animal had left his calling card for me. Right on my trail was a big pile of wolf poop!

Well that was rude, but I was the intruder in his area I guess and that was the best message he could send me. Back at camp I hung the animals up and got myself a coffee. Remembering to grab a # 4 Longspring trap I made my way back across the lake and set the trap right where the bait stealing wolves kept stepping over a small log near the cubby. Wiring it to the step over log I covered it with a light layer of dry grass and snow. That should work if they come back tonight again.

Back in camp I went about my evening rituals. Cup of coffee, supper, coffee, skinning, coffee, stretching and finally off to bed. Oh, I forgot, one more coffee, some writing and some music before sleep time.

(November 20)

I awoke to my first Northern Ontario blizzard. The wind was driving snow parallel to the ground and stinging the side of my face as I hurried to check the wolf set. Getting close I realized that if there was one in the trap I would have been able to see it from where I was. Maybe they hadn't come back with the storm. Bending down to clear of some of the snow that had fallen I noticed a piece of wire sticking up out of the snow. Pulling on it I followed it right to the step over log. The trap was gone! I didn't grasp what had happened for a minute. But closer inspection of the wire showed that the wolf had got caught and had chewed right through it.

Are you kidding me? In eight hours it had come, got caught, and got out. There were bite marks all the way to the end of the heavy stove wire. The wolf, now with a trap on its foot, and its partner had gone into the bush right behind the set and come back out on the lake about fifty yards away. There I lost the trail in the drifting, windblown snow. Man what a bummer! Not only did I lose a trap and a wolf, now that animal will suffer and that was really not what I wanted. Boy, the strength and cunning of these animals were amazing.

But for now I had better get back and get some breakfast in me before my trip down the Pody Lake trails. Bannock, oatmeal, coffee and tang should be enough to get me over the trail and back again. Cutting up the frozen beaver carcass for bait Lobo gulped down the chunks of meat that flew off. Finally, with the shoes strapped on my feet and the pack on my back, we were on the road again.

At the second trap of the day a problem presented itself to me, in the form of a nice male marten that was so frozen that I could not get the trap of the body without taking the chance of damaging the fur. I needed to carry spare traps with me and having had only two spare 120's, I came to realize that once my 220's were set I would be out of the trap setting business for awhile. I was hoping that when I brought my fur out on Dec 23rd I could send it away and order more traps from the O.T.A.'s trap sales department. So dropping my pack I hurried back to camp and grabbed the two spare traps along with a couple of 220's.

Finally back on point, I moved down the trail and wondered to myself if there was a tree full of 120 conibears left anywhere for me. At the beaver house the dam was now frozen solid so I pulled the trap and put the rock and the wire on the shore for next year. I never left anything on the dam because the beavers would just use it as building material. Taking the trail to Pody Lake first I caught a flying squirrel, a red squirrel and a marten in the four traps.

Standing on the ice of Pody Lake, I decided that instead of backtracking I would follow the river down to Little Pody Lake and make myself a nice circle trail. For the most part the river was quite large and I had no need to worry about thin ice. There were but a few small fast water areas that I had to detour around, so at those spots I set the 220's for marten. I did find one beaver house but having forgotten to throw some snares into my pocket I left it for the next trip. The odd fox track, mink tracks and tons of otter tracks were all up and down the river. The otters had their toilets at each of the open water areas and it looked like they came back to the same place time and time again to do their business. Just after the third portage area the river started to widen out and take a turn to the east. There I noticed a creek coming in from the south and decided to explore that in the future.

But once again I had travelled that far and not seen one marten track crossing the river in any kind of open area. It had to be that they were afraid of predators. And I bet it was those Great Grey owls that they were worried about. Following the north shore of the lake I kept watch for beaver houses without finding anything at all. Fifteen minutes later I was on my trail heading north towards camp. The first trap was the mink set where I had tried to get a shot at the mink. I could see that the trap was not in place so grabbing the wire I was happy to see the dark brown fur of a nice mink pop out of the snow. Next was the dam gateway set where all the otter tracks had been. I had high hopes for an otter but had to settle for a big beaver instead.

Hooking up my drag line I made it back to camp with some actual daylight left and just one more squirrel in the bag. This had been another good day other than the wolf situation and the wind. Thinking about supper I grabbed the water pail and went down to check my fish lines. The three pound northern that was on one of the lines would make a nice couple of meals for me along with some bannock. The lake was cool looking with wave after wave of drifted snow piled up. Driven by the north wind it had really made high drifts in the narrows. Looked neat but wasn't going to be much fun walking through them.

Getting supper out of the way before I started my chores I decided to spread my traps out a little bit. If I pulled one out of every four sets I would have boxes and traps to expand into more area. I really needed to get traps out to Scuckasu Lake as the bush between there and Ahmabel Lake would be a natural funnel for the marten. And after buying more traps I could fill the spots back in with more boxes. Perfect, I would start tomorrow with my new plan.

Inside for the night I jumped on my daily chores. Skinning, stretching, if I had a beaver removing the fat for my oil lamps and stripping some meat off the back legs for jerky. Finally some radio time, a coffee and a journal entry and it was lights out.

(November 21)

It was the 21st and that made three weeks in the bush so far. A month and two days till the plane would arrive for my pickup. Still loving it but maybe by that time I would miss talking to other people. Ya right! For now however my routine stayed the same. Check my traps, expand my area and try to fill my fur bag. Figuring to pull the mink trap from the point and six other sets on the way to Ahmabel I should be able to get a nice line set past the lake. Maybe even to Scuckasu, and East Ahmabel.

But that would defiantly mean spending two nights at the Ahmabel camp. Making sure to pack a blanket to help guard against the night cold I threw a few 220's in the pack and a bunch of beaver snares. With breakfast cooked and my last cup of coffee drained I loaded up. Snowshoes on and packsack shouldered I stepped away from the cabin.

Stopping to pull the mink set I was surprised to see two wolf tracks back and the bait stolen again. One wolf was obviously dragging a trap. Now that was just an insult, and running back to the cabin, I left the dog there (because I did not need him getting involved in this) and grabbed my 30.06. I was going wolf hunting! After all how far and fast could it run with a trap on its foot?

Well that was something I was about to find out. Following the tracks north along the lake shore they cut into the bush about three hundred yards from the point. There they took off into the bush on the east side of the lake and only fifty feet in I came across two very fresh beds. They had just taken off before I got there. Now the chase was on, and on and on! Pointed in a generally east direction I trailed them at the fastest possible speed through some terribly rough country.

The wolf with the trap was always in the rear, the other one breaking trail for it and as the day progressed we were pulling circles and back tracking and at one point came out on Chain lake 7 where they ran down to the south end of the lake and back in the bush to the west again. And always old trap-paw was behind. Was he just following the other one or was the front wolf purposefully breaking trail for him. Either way it was amazing that for that many miles I trailed them and never got even a glimpse.

The hours passed by and the circles kept getting tighter and tighter until they were only one hundred yards across. They stayed in the thickest bush they could find and finally the inevitable happened. The wolves had jumped across a three foot crevasse in the rocks and as I jumped over the tail of my snowshoe was on one side and the toe on the other somehow and snap. The left shoe broke right in half. This was a disappointing end to the chase, and as I limped my way home with the day totally shot I mused about the pain in my neck that these two wolves turned out to be. But one thing did come of it. Those two wolves with the telltale track were never seen again that year.

Knowing that I was still between Hiawatha and Chain Lakes I headed straight west, limping along on my broken snowshoe. After a short time I came out on Hiawatha Lake just at the start of the narrows, six hours later and only a hundred yards from where I had went into the bush. Grabbing my pack from where I had dropped it at the point I worked my way back to camp. I made an early supper of the left over fish and some bannock. With no skinning to do I took some time to care for the pelts that were in the fur bags and on the stretchers. It is a pleasure to take each fur and clean any grease or dirt, brushing it out and remembering the circumstances of many of the catches.

Finally with everything taken care of I turned on the radio and jotted down the days happenings. With a cup of coffee I relaxed in bed and eventually blew out the beaver fat lamp. Dreams of wolves filled my head and when morning rolled around I woke up, pissed off at the animals in general.

TO THE NORTHERN BOUNDARY

(November 22)

With my meal finished and a coffee in hand I took down my long distance snowshoes. These ones were 66" long by 14" wide where the regular shoes are 48" by 14". The smaller ones are easier to maneuver through the bush, but until I had a plan on how to fix them, I would just use my big ones. Checking the lamp wick bindings on these shoes (because I would prefer to change them in the warm cabin if I had to), they were fine so I set them outside to cool down and loaded up my pack again.

Down the hill I went, still grumbling about those wolves and Lobo followed silently along behind me sensing my mood I guess. But it didn't last long. How could anyone stay upset on a day like today and in a place like this? They had outsmarted me fair and square and it probably would not be the last time that happened. As long as I got to win a few rounds every once in awhile, life would be good.

Turning north as I hit the lake I totally ignored the point. I didn't even want to know if they had come back last night. At the north end of the lake I picked up my mink trap, and figuring that I could add a couple of boxes to my load, I decided to take a few from along the river as they were not producing as good as the overland sets were. My first trap was sprung but the second had a good marten in it. But something looked odd on the box. I thought it was a squirrel sitting there but as I got closer out of the box popped a marten. I guess he was head down in the box chewing on the frozen bait and it was his tail that I saw sticking up. He flew up the tree and with this being my first live marten encounter I was amazed at how fast the thing could climb. No wonder they could catch squirrels in the trees. They were much faster than the little rodents.

Changing the trap over, the marten just watched from his perch thirty feet over my head. I would no doubt have him in my trap on the return trip. I had brought a limited amount of bait today since I was counting on catching a beaver or two in my sets. Once I got to the Little Fraser River I checked my otter traps and was disappointed to see otter tracks climbing from the water and going around my now frozen traps. The ice had formed where the steel and water met with open water in front and behind the trap. Must be the cold transferring through the steel that had started the ice forming! I would have to figure out away to set the otter traps completely under water.

For now I just knocked the ice off and figured out a plan for the future. I noticed a large shadow float by and looking up I saw my old friend the Great Grey owl. He landed on the top of a broken off dead tree and all but disappeared. I didn't know if they are that smart that they know or it was just a fluke, but landing there he looked just like a continuation of the tree. Perfect camo, no wonder the marten didn't come out in the open at all.

Adding a mink, a marten and a squirrel to my pack I left them hanging by a wire in a sheltered tree to be picked up on the way back. Turning left I made my way up the mile of trail to Third Otter Lake. Again the otter trap was frozen but my 330 was filled with a huge beaver. Hooking it up to my drag line I returned to pick up my pack and boxes that I had left at the junction of the trails. Pointing myself east I crossed Otter Lake and hit the Ahmabel trail. My first cubby netted me a good marten and reaching the beaver snare set I crouched down, cleared the snow of the crystal clear ice, and swung my axe.

What the heck? But it was too late. Did I really see what I thought I saw? Carefully chopping around the edge of the ice hole I pulled the snare pole up and yes it was. An otter had got caught in the snare and almost reached the surface of the water. Dying there his face was frozen into the ice and my first axe swing had put a deep gash in his face. Thank goodness it wasn't in his back where the price would really have dropped. Weird though, an otter in a beaver bait set. He must have just been swimming by and passed to close to the pole. Cool, I'll take it!

"Keep going Dave" I said to myself. "You still have a long ways to go" but when I got to my crawl over log I remember that at that point I was only about a quarter of a mile from the lake. It was a little more difficult to get over the log with my long snowshoes on but I managed with a small ballet step and carried on. By the time I hit the lake another marten was included and I was thinking that this was a pretty good day. The cabin beckoned me and my stomach answered, sure I'll stop for a coffee and a bite to eat.

Building a fire I placed the beaver in a spot where the fur could dry before skinning. That done I dug into my pack and pulled out my last can of stew. With my belt knife I opened the lid of the can and it was frozen. I emptied the contents with the help of my knife and a big spoon and soon the thick gravy was bubbling away. With a big chunk of bannock to soak up the juice I dove in. Blah! The veggies and potatoes had turned into a half solid watery mush type of food. Might be ok for someone with no teeth but it was gross to me.

But still, what choice did I have? I gulped it down without chewing anything but the meat and washed it all down with some hot coffee. Well that was good to know. Frozen canned food was disgusting. Something to remember for the future! Filling up the stove I headed out to set the beaver house just around the corner and take a trip up the Fraser River if I had time. Adding a marten box on the portage over to the river I made it back to camp having set three beaver, one mink and a marten trap.

With my trusty coffee in hand I decided it was skinning time. Starting on the beaver I got the skin peeled off and after cutting the castors out I rolled them up in the skin to be brought back to Hiawatha where they would be stretched and dried. The other animals were still not thawed so I guessed they could wait till the morning to get taken care of. With a little more bannock and jam as a bedtime snack I made myself ready for another uncomfortable night of half sleep and half fill the darn wood stove!

GET LOST MUCH?

(November 23)

Ok, so apparently I should have brought two sleeping bags into the bush with me. This whole mattress for a blanket deal would get old real fast. With the stove roaring and the water on I jumped back into bed till it warmed up somewhat. The temperature must have dropped outside because it had sure dropped in here. I wasn't sure what the "R" value of one half inch plywood was but I was willing to bet it wasn't much. Not sure how I was going to be able to sleep in here when it got to be forty below but I knew it wouldn't be much fun.

I would say it was only around the zero mark and I was already feeling frozen when I woke up... for the fifth time. But you know nothing warms a guy up like a good walk so after cornmeal pancakes and fried beaver meat for breakfast I headed off for Scuckasu Lake.

Passing the beaver set that I had made last night and continuing on past the river mouth where I had seen the otter on the last trip, I turned left up the final bay and arrived at my jump off point. It was only a half a mile through the bush to Scuckasu Lake and I had already dialed in my compass for the trip. For that short of a trip I didn't really need to keep that close of an eye on the compass so just checking every once in a while I moved along. Blazing every twenty feet or so I slowly travelled along, watching for fur sign and seeing quite a bit of marten tracks.

Soon enough I realized that I should have been at the lake by now. I had been moving for a good hour and even with the constant blazing I should have hit the lake. I had been aiming for the south east corner of the lake and thought maybe I had drifted a little east of my target. At this point I stopped blazing because I figured I was going to have to straighten the trail out anyway. Estimating that I must be somewhere between the lake to the west and the river to the east, I turned myself straight west on the compass and went that way.

After another hour had passed I really started questioning what I had done. Maybe I really hadn't travelled far enough north, so I turned that way. But now I was not sure of anything. I could always just follow my tracks back but that meant the last few hours were wasted and then I let my stubborn side kick in. I went this way and then that way until finally I started checking the compass closely. I would take a reading and move fifty feet and take another one. The compass was pointing in a totally different direction. Great I had been compassing over a magnetic anomaly in the rocks here.

Now what? Sitting down and taking stock I tried my best to figure out where I might be. Lobo looked at me like I would have been looking at him if he was leading this expedition. It was only an educated guess but my instincts told me I was west of the lake. It could not be the east side I was on because I would have been in a big circle with the lake on one side and the rivers on two other sides. My tracks would have closed the circle and with the amount of walking that I had done I would have hit one of those landmarks.

So the west it had to be! Turning east I walked for what I felt was the max distance I needed to cover before I should have hit the lake and then not having found it I turned south. This was all done having put the unreliable compass away and using the sun for directions. After a fifteen minute walk I saw the bush open up and there I was. Standing on the shore line of Scuckasu Lake! The northwest shore that is! I was on the exact opposite side of the lake that I had been aiming for. Boy my cross-country racing coach at school would have been proud.

But the point was I was there, and like I always said "I have never been lost, but I did get turned around for two days once". With this day better than two thirds gone I traveled south along the west shoreline looking for beaver houses. Nothing! Again a lake that has all the poplar trees cut far back into the bush. I arrived at my intended access point to this lake and noticed a big lump under the snow. Could it be a beaver house? Checking, it was just a boat. What? Just a boat what the heck was a boat doing here? Looking up I saw a blaze on a tree just inside the bush line. Oh man, you have got to be kidding me. But sure enough there was another blaze just further in a little ways. And another and yes you guessed it, a whole line of them, with a ten foot wide trail following along. Walking along shaking my head in disbelief I broke out onto Ahmabel Lake about seventy five yards from where I had started this trail so many hours ago. The start of the trail was hidden by a big upturned tree.

Well that was certainly an almost total waste of time. And I say almost because at least in the end I did find the trail. Might have been nice to know it was there before I started though." Whatever", I thought to myself and stepped out onto the lake. I'll just go check my traps that I set last night and then cut some firewood. Lobo decided it was time for him to start walking on the tail end of my snowshoes and I turned and give him the look. He knows I hated it when he did that. He glanced sheepishly from side to side as if to say "Sorry boss, my mistake".

Stopping to pull a beaver from the set, I dragged it back to camp and rebuilt the fire. I was so bummed at how the day had gone I almost convinced myself to head back to Hiawatha and my nice warm sleeping bag. And maybe this cabin did look nicer than my dugout, but this camp had nothing on mine for staying warm. But thankfully with only a couple hours of daylight left, common sense prevailed and I stayed put till morning. Not that I am afraid of the dark but it just wasn't a safe time to be travelling at this time of the year.

Supper consisted of more of the same, and while relaxing over a cup of coffee, I noted that on the next trip I needed to bring coffee with me as the supply here would be gone by morning. Outside I cut a couple of trees and killed the last hour of the day bucking it up with the saw that was hanging in the shed. Back inside with the warmth getting to me I daydreamed about hamburgers and french-fries with a big bottle of coke to wash it all down. I meant no disrespect to the guy who invented cornmeal but the problem was it tasted just like cornmeal.

Tiring of wiping the drool from my chin I loaded the stove, crawled between the blankets and readied myself for another crappy night. This time however I took another mattress and stood it up behind me to hopefully add a little windbreak for my back. It seemed to help as I drifted off, only to awaken every two to three hours to fill the stove. Finally I saw the eastern sky starting to lighten up. Thank you lord! It's time to go!

(November 24)

By the time the sun was fully over the horizon I was half a mile down Ahmabel Lake and making tracks for the south. At my trail head I turned west and took a second to reset a sprung trap. Removing a squirrel from the next set I kept an eye out for fresh sign along the way. Passing Otter Lake I declined turning north to Third Otter and continued toward camp.

My wolf snares were still set so I pushed them aside for Lobo to pass and replaced them. The next trap held a marten and I replaced the trap, moving on without wasting too much time. A little further I saw a set of tracks and as I got closer I was surprised that it was a marten that had ventured out into the open. He walked out about twenty feet then highballed it back into the bush with his telltale two track running formation. These traps that I had set along the wide grassy areas were a waste of time and I decided to move them and concentrate my sets in the areas where the bush was right up to the river. These places, I at least saw a few regular marten tracks.

Sounds good, I mused to myself as I moved across the ground, my snowshoes eating up the miles. Another marten and a weasel/ ermine were added before I hit the crossover trail. Ermine, like Snowshoe hares turn white during the winter for protection when the snow is on the ground. I remembered the last winter down south when we had a good snowfall but then in December it rained for several days. I was out checking traps and the poor rabbits were huddled under the spruce trees trying to stay dry. With the snow totally gone they looked like white targets everywhere, and after taking a couple I just gave up. It wasn't even fair. The rest I just watched as I walked by. They thought they were so invisible.

But here there was no shortage of snow and not a rabbit to hide anyway, unless they were really good at hiding, and had learned to fly, hence the lack of tracks. I didn't think this was too likely but as I was approaching the trail to Hiawatha I noticed a spot where a grouse had dove into the snow. But I could not see where it had emerged from its hole. I had encountered this before so very slowly I moved forward. Finally I noticed a slightly darker spot of snow and jumping suddenly on top of it the grouse was trapped under my snowshoes. Knowing that it was going to try and move sideways I watched to pick a spot and as it broke from the snow I smothered it in my arms. Grabbing it by the neck I gave it a snap and it was over for this bird. Cool, supper again! The odd thing was that they normally do this on the colder nights and then are gone at daylight. I had never seen one under the snow at this time of the day before. But oh well! His laziness was my dinner. At the trail head I was watching for my owl buddies when I noticed a black spot in the bush to the west. Actually there were several and they turned out to be moose. Three or four that I could tell, but they moved in and out of the tree line browsing along as they went and so it was hard to pinpoint their numbers.

I watched them until they disappeared and I continued on my way. That started me to wondering why I had not noticed any wolf kills yet since there was a lot of moose and more than enough wolves. I wondered what they were eating then, besides my bait I mean.

Dropping my pack I followed in the same direction the moose went since my beaver trap was in the same area. Arriving at the set I chopped around the trap poles and once loose I gave the set a lift. Right on, definitely something heavy in there so I started cutting a big enough hole to get a beaver out. It wouldn't move so I tried again but still no go. Clearing the slush out of the hole I knelt down and looked into the water. Ah I see! Chop some more, try again, chop some more and finally with a good pull I am the proud owner of a six foot poplar log. Not too sure what the fur of this thing was worth so I decided to practice catch and release with this one.

Resetting, I turned and headed back to my pack. Lobo greeted me from his bed where he had curled up and went to sleep. Getting up, he gave me a tail wag. I just looked at him and said "Ya, whatever dog, have a good sleep?" But I guess I hadn't really needed his help anyway. He never had been much good with an axe.

The first two traps toward Hiawatha were sprung, one with Whiskey jack feathers in it but the last one had a nice big marten. The animal was still partially alive so I squeezed its heart until it expired. It took only a few seconds to finish the animal off, so I removed it and replaced the trap.

Finally I was back on Hiawatha! It seemed like I had been gone for days. The wind had drifted snow over my trail and it was only visible in a few places. Following along, slipping off the trail here and there I came upon the tracks of that huge wolf again. He came out of the bush from the west and followed my trail south down the lake. He had more luck following the trail than I had been having. Walking along I tried to count how many beaver houses I had found. Not very many compared to down south where there was much more food and a lot less predators. Looking at the bush around here I was sure a lumber company would do very well, but I really hoped that they would never make it in this far.

The wolf followed my trail right to where I turned right to go to the camp. There he fidgeted around a little but finally went left and I went right. Happily I climbed the hill that marked me being home, and happy I was to be there. Crawling backwards into the cabin I dragged my pack in with me. My first order of business was to get a fire going. Some birch bark, a few pieces of kindling and a match, and voila, we had fire. It didn't take long for the heat to begin radiating from the thin tin walls of the stove.

Throwing a few bigger chunks on I set the pail near the stove and put my coffee pot on. When the pail has loosened up a bit I smashed the ice and left it to thaw. Waiting for the water to boil gave me time to get my catch prepared for thawing and stretching. Soon the water was boiling and a wonderful hot cup of this heavenly, life giving brew was ready for me. Removing pelts, stretching and skinning kept me busy for the next few hours, taking a break long enough to have a delicious meal of grouse and bannock dipped in grouse gravy. Yum-yum!

With my chores finished I went outside to answer Mother Nature and heard a strange kind of humming coming from the south. With no wind at all the sound carried and weirdly enough it sounded like a train. Could I hear a train from twenty plus miles away? I had no idea but there was no other explanation for it so that is what I decided it was. Boy, that sound could really carry on a cold clear night like this.

With all the miles I had put on in the last few days I decided to stay in camp the next day, kickback a little and replace my firewood pile. With the weather turning steadily colder I was using a lot more wood. I decided to cut a bunch of green birch wood also because it should last a lot longer than straight dry wood. With my day all planned out I crawled into my bed and it was so nice compared to the mattress sandwich I had slept on the night before.

Falling asleep with a little good night music I was awakened by Lobo's frantic barking. The cabin was half filled with smoke and the wall above the stove pipe was on fire. I had forgotten to shut the stove down and the bark on the log had ignited. Rushing I threw cup after cup of water until there was not a hint of a spark left. Opening the door it took but a few minutes for the smoke to clear and I was none the worse for wear. But hey! Thanks again there dog!

CHRISTMAS IS A MONTH AWAY

(November 25)

Waking, I laid there and realized that it was just one month till Christmas. And that also meant one month minus two days till pick-up time. Crawling from my bed to the stove, I set about getting ready for chow. With breakfast on the way, a coffee in hand and a slow relaxing day ahead of me, I figured life was good.

Once outside I noticed the temperature had come up. Twenty two degrees above zero, and the snow was starting to fall. Right behind the camp were three nice birch trees that I had been peeling for fire starter and they were my first victims. My axe took them down in short order and I buck sawed them into ten foot pieces. Even at that length they were all a person could manage on his shoulder. With all three trees back at camp I was wishing for some box horses to cut the wood on. I was getting tired of sawing from my knees.

Two large Jack pine trees that were about four feet apart stood beside the camp. Looking at them I thought that they might make a good set of box horses. I cut them off about four feet from the ground and with my saw I cut the tops of the stumps into V shapes that the logs could sit in and be solid. From there I would just cut a stove length off one end and then one off the opposite end until the piece was only four feet long. The last two cuts would still have to be made from the ground but it was sure easier cutting standing up this way. Happy with my invention I retrieved more birch trees from behind the cabin and then started on a dry wood supply.

On one of the trips down to the lake shore for dry wood I decide to check the trap across the lake on the point. Cool, a nice marten was added to my catch and I had not even planned on catching anything today. But since I forgot to bring a trap with me I had to make a return trip to get a conibear back into the box.

Cut some more trees, buck them up and stop for a coffee and some supper. With a little daylight left I took a run behind camp to check the two closest marten traps. The second trap had a marten or at least what's left of one. Wolves had been there, knocked the box from the tree, stolen the bait and eaten all of the marten except what was between the jaws of the trap. That's it, tomorrow there would be a # 4 longspring trap waiting for their return. But this time it would be anchored properly.

The wolves left the set following my trail so I followed hoping they had not repeated their dastardly deeds again. No worries, they turned off the trail well before the next trap and a good thing because it held a female marten. Should I continue or head back to camp? Camp it was and I would check this line in the morning. Back at the cabin I started splitting the pile of fire wood that I had sawn. Just the big pieces though and as the sun set behind the trees to the west my firewood pile was quite impressive for just using an axe and a bucksaw.

Tossing a bunch into the open doorway I decided to spend some time tonight fixing my snowshoe. I really didn't want to use my big shoes tomorrow so I got to work on it. The break was just back of the crossbeam so I took two pieces of kindling and shape them into the same thickness as the actual frame. Then putting a six inch spike on the inside I wired the wood and nail tightly to the frame itself. With both sides done the same I finished by wrapping the entire brace with nylon string. Hopefully this would hold and the test would come tomorrow.

This project had taken up a couple of hours so now I could get at the fur that was ready to skin. The insides of the marten were still frozen but they were just thawed enough to get the pelt off the carcass. After getting the stretching done I was finished for the night. I mixed up a final cup of coffee and with the radio on I caught up on my journal entries. Finally with the light blown out I drifted off, travelling the trails with Chick Ferguson from the book Mink, Mary and Me and with Jim Vander Beck from Traplines North.

(November 26)

It felt good to wake up and not have that cold breeze coming in through the door where it "almost" met the wall. The temperature must have risen during the night. Outside for my morning ritual I checked the thermometer and sure enough it was just below the freezing point. It should be a nice day for a walk, with the three or four inches of fresh snow from yesterday and last night. It was always great heading out on the first trip after a snow. You know that all the tracks you will see are going to be very fresh.

I was hoping to get to the north end of Pody Lake today and maybe even up the east creek for a ways also. With my breakfast of oatmeal and bannock finished I strapped on my shoes and was off. My pack was loaded with all my requirements for the day like spare traps, wire, bait, axe, snares and oh yes; let's add that wolf trap right now. Nothing in the first two sets so I cut a pole about five inches thick and ten feet long to attach the trap to. Placing the trap where the wolves would have to step if they came to steal my bait again, I covered it with loose snow, placed a few guide sticks and moved on down the trail.

By the time I reached the beaver house at Little Pody Lake I had added a squirrel and a marten to my pack. Checking the beaver set I pulled a small beaver out of the trap with a minimum delay. Stepping out onto the lake ice I was greeted by the sight of four otters travelling east across the lake. They were headed for the mouth of Pody Creek where it flowed out toward Nagagami Lake barely a mile from where I stood. They were so cool to watch as they would run a few hops and then slide for five or six feet. I had seen their tracks doing this many times but had never witnessed it in person. So cool!

Watching until they disappeared, I pointed my nose west and followed the lake shore until I hit the creek entrance. There I went into the bush to look for a spot to set a #220 conibear for marten. Cutting a six inch tree about twenty feet long I wired the pole to another tree about six feet from the ground. I needed the small end of the pole to be about six feet past the second tree. Nailing a piece of bait at the very end of the pole I then nailed a six inch long stick that was about an inch or so thick across the main pole about a foot from the bait. Next I squeezed the trap onto the cross stick and wired the chain to the main pole. Covering the entire set with spruce boughs, to hide the bait from birds, and to form a sort of cubby with the only opening being through the trap, the set was complete. It was basically the same as the leaning pole sets but just with the pole parallel to the ground. A little more work than the leaning pole but I just wanted to see which method worked better.

Surveying my handy work I decided it looked good, but I guessed that the martens would be the final judge of that. Putting two more of these sets along the river and making a beaver snare set at the house I had found on the last trip, took up a bit of my spare time. When I finally reached the trail back to Hiawatha I figured I might still have a hour or two for exploring, so cruising along the western shore I kept watch for a live house. I had noticed that on most of the lakes the beavers had a tendency to build their lodges on the west shore. Not sure why but my thinking was that they didn't build on the shore where the waves were normally hitting.

The lake was very picturesque with many tiny islands and with a nice rock face shoreline in many places. Passing several houses that I checked out for sign of life I saw nothing alive until I hit the very end of the lake. There were some fox, mink and of course the ever present moose tracks along the lake shore, but again not much food for the beavers. I quickly threw in a snare bait set at the house and then a marten trap in the bush a short distance behind. This side of Pody Lake would be a whole new marten area since they wouldn't cross the lake and I was only a half mile from the western boundary of my trap line. And I was fairly certain there was no one trapping over there. Moving back south I followed the east shore until I came to the creek that flowed in from the east.

This was the creek that almost joined up with the headwaters of the Little Fraser River and would eventually become one of my circle trails. Putting a marten set just in the bush line I followed the creek and found another house a half mile upstream from the lake. With a good entrance visible I dropped a 330 in front of it and added a bait set before I hurried on my way. Again I had pushed the day a little too long and I would be walking back in the dark once more. Lobo seemed unconcerned since he'd had all the rest he needed. Every time I stopped to make a set he curled up and slept. But I guess he was just along to save my life when I needed him to, which seemed to be more often than I liked. You would think I would have been used to this walking after dark deal but it was just such a pain getting home and unpacking everything in the dark.

I was moving a little slower than normal with the beaver dragging behind me, and with one more marten added to the pack, I finally saw the outline of the cabin, a welcoming tiny spiral of smoke still escaping from the chimney. Once supper was finished I checked the beaver and it was dry enough to skin. Twenty minutes later with the beaver skinned out the marten were all still to frozen, so I stripped the fat off the beaver carcass and sliced some of the meat up for jerky. One quarter inch strips soaked in salt water overnight, and in the morning they would be hung to dry over the stove pipe.

Setting the frying pan full of beaver fat on the stove, I kept an eye on it while I stretched the beavers pelt and then took care of skinning the squirrels and the marten. With all my chores done I took the frying pan off the stove, grabbed a coffee and stepped outside for some fresh air. It was a beautiful night and as I sat on the woodpile, sipping on my coffee I just couldn't believe how lucky I was. A kid from down south who had dreamed of this for years and here I was. No matter how many times I thought about it, it just didn't seem real. Even though some times the daily routine would get a little hum-drum there was always the excitement of the next trap. I was having the time of my life!

Relaxing with my back against the cabin wall I heard far off in the southern distance a lone wolf howling. Could it be that giant that I had followed up Hiawatha Lake? It sounded like it was coming from Nagagami Lake or at least close to it. But where ever it was it was a perfect end to a wonderful day. Crawling back inside I finished up my nightly rituals, radio, journal and a coffee. I know, how did I sleep with that much coffee right? Well I have always said "Sleep is for people who have nothing better to do".

A MOOSE IN A STEW

(November 27)

Morning broke nice and mild. Mild was ok as long as it stayed below the freezing mark. First things first, I needed a coffee! While waiting for the water to boil I took a minute to flip the marten pelts to fur side out. Breakfast that morning was cornmeal pancakes with some jam on them. I was spreading the jam a little thin these days as it was on the verge of extinction. At least in my neck of the woods it was. Sugar and several other items had also started getting scarce, but I never said I was a pro at estimating how much food I would be needing for this trip, and besides, I couldn't have gotten much more on the plane if I had brought it with me anyway. The sugar probably would have been fine except for the fact that some days I would get home and crave sweets so bad that I would eat a couple spoons of sugar straight, which seemed to deplete my supply rather quickly. Weird hey, but thankfully the cravings had subsided as of late.

Today I was off to Chain Lakes. Remembering an extra drag rope for Lobo because I was sure his help would be needed today with all the beaver sets that I needed to check. Loading my pack I strapped on my shoes and was off on the days travels. Out on the lake the coat opened up the hat came off as well as the mitts. Twenty eight degrees made for some warm walking and I didn't want to get too sweated up right away.

Passing the point it came to mind that I had not seen the tracks of the wolf with the trap on its foot since my wild goose (wolf)

110

chase awhile back. I felt bad for that animal but he should have left while he had the chance. Maybe he would jump into one of my snares at some point. And that made me realize something. So far I had been reacting to the wolves instead of setting snares and letting them come to me. I vowed to set whatever snares I had with me and get the rest of the ones in camp out there. They were not going to catch anything hanging on the wall. Thinking about where I would set my snares almost made me walk right past my fox set at the bottom of the lake. And glad I hadn't or I would have had to wait to see the gorgeous Red Fox that lay there tangled in the willows. Gosh he was a beautiful specimen with thick, dark red fur that just shone in the sunlight.

A great start! Pumped for the day now I hurried to the trail head and climbing the hill I saw a big dark marten hanging in the conibear. Love it! My next set had a nice buck mink in the trap. Funny though, we were a long way from water and it was quite a bit early for them to be running around on the prowl for a girl friend. Guess he was just a wanderer. With the emphasis being on "was".

Feeling very good about my early catch I arrived at Lake Three with a decision to make, north first, or south? Just for a change I took north. Slipping along the trail I realized that maybe the traps were producing so well today because I had not been here in a week. By the time I reached Lake Six I had another marten and two squirrels added to the load. Leaving Lake Six I cruised along the grassy flats and rounding the second bend I noticed four moose standing on the opposite bush line. Looked like a cow and three calves, or at least three smaller moose. But that couldn't be, I had never read anything about moose having triplets.

Very cool anyway and I moved slowly along watching them as they stared back at me. They were milling around like they didn't want to leave when I noticed something on the ice ahead of me. At first glance I thought it was an otter or a beaver and I saw mud thrown up all over the ice. But as I got closer, to my surprise it turned out to be a cow moose. She had fallen through the ice and become stuck in the mud of the almost dry creek bed. She looked at me pleadingly or maybe it was just fear, but whatever it was she was the saddest animal I had ever come across.

Her front legs were up on the ice and her knees were scraped raw from trying to pull her weight out of the quicksand like "Loonshit" mud. Struggling momentarily as I arrived, she soon settled down and I studied this problem. The bottom seemed endless because it looked like she was standing up or maybe her back hooves were touching solid bottom. Maybe if I cut some poles she could get enough leverage to pull out of the mud. Dropping my pack I went to shore cut a couple of trees down and dragged them out on the ice. Trimming the branches off and throwing them in the mud I took the poles and slid them under her front legs. With her struggling to get out and me prying with the poles she seemed to move a little bit. But her strength was so far gone she would fight for a minute and then just sink back into the mud.

Lobo just sat there staring at me as if to say "Hey dummy, you are short of food and..." But I just couldn't bring myself to kill this poor thing. She had fought so hard to get out it would be a shame to come along and just kill her. For hours I worked at getting her out of there. Sliding more and more logs under her until I finally tried putting my drag line around her neck and pulling her. The moose never even flinched as I set the noose around her neck although she did struggle somewhat when the noose tightened a little.

Finally, with the sun down behind the trees, my traps not checked and me still better than two hours from home I had to leave. I decided to come back the next day to try again since I still had to check my traps anyway. So pointing my snowshoes south I made tracks at a fast clip. It seemed weird to me that a moose would venture out on thin ice like that and my next thought was that at least I was not the only thing in this area stupid enough to fall through the ice. Small consolation though because I'm quite sure that I was supposed to be more intelligent than a moose. Walking by the light of a less than quarter moon I crossed lake after lake until I hit the trail west to Hiawatha. Here the thick forest closed in around me and the thick spruce blocked out what little light there was.

Slow and easy was the order of the day as I made my way along the trail. I had travelled in the bush after dark often enough down south that I knew that as long as you took your time you should be ok. I remembered one night trip down south where I had been about to step on this big rock when it moved under my foot. Turned out the rock was a porcupine! Ya, I had to change my underwear when I got home. But this trip went by uneventfully, and I was happy to see the bush open up as Hiawatha Lake came into view.

A short time later with my catch hung to thaw I sat with a coffee and tried to figure a solution to my moose problem. I had about one hundred and fifty feet of rope with me and if I could reach the shore with that I could climb a big tree and tie the rope up high with the other end around the moose's neck. By cutting the tree down so it fell away from the moose the weight should help pull it out of the water. Either that or strangle it I guess! That was probably a mute point anyway because I didn't think that was enough rope to reach the shore. But I would carry it with me anyway, just in case.

With a half assed plan in my mind I left the animals hanging, turned down the stove and hit the sack. During the night a cold breeze stirred my sleep and I rolled over thinking to myself "The weather has turned."

(November 28)

Dawn caught me a mile down the lake. The weather had definitely turned as the thermometer had dropped by twenty five degrees. With the sun just starting to peak over the horizon right above my trail to Chain Lakes the temperature was probably forced down another five degrees or so. The next few miles went by quickly as I hurried to try and get my plan into action. Rounding the last corner I knew right away that I was too late.

Her head was just out of the water and the open area was now frozen over with the cold temperatures. The freezing water had finally sapped the last bit of heat from her massive body. I felt so bad that this animal had to die like this but that is nature I guess. This, or torn apart by wolves, either way that is the life of a moose in the north.

Nothing left to do now but try and salvage what I could from her. She had sunk deep into the mud but with an hour of prying and pulling I was able to get to a point where I could cut her left front quarter off. With one of the poles I had cut the day before I chopped a hole in the ice and stuck the pole down into the mud as far as I could get it. With the rope tied to her hoof and the other end around the pole for added leverage, I cut and pulled till the huge mass of meat and hide came apart from the rest of her. As it let go the remainder slid back into the water with just her head sticking out.

Taking an hour to separate the muscles from the bone and skin I piled it on shore until I returned from my traps. At Lake 7 a marten awaited my arrival and hurrying on to my beaver set on Lake 8 I chopped through the few inches of ice and lifted the pole. Good weight there must be a big beaver! Chopping the hole big enough to get a beaver out I lifted and was surprised to see a little beaver. Well it sure felt heavier than that so I pulled the pole all the way out and was doubly surprised to see a second beaver caught in the same snare set. That had never happened to me before. I had caught two muskrats in an entrance set before. I guess they had been racing to get out of the house. They both had lost!

Hooking up my drag line I remembered first to check my marten set at the end of the lake. Yes another marten! I had forgotten to bring a spare trap but with some prying I managed to get the trap off and reset it. I was standing at the junction of a creek that flowed in from the east. This would be my access point to the Fraser River system. The trip would be about four miles along the creek, then overland, and then down another creek to the lake, to finally be able to hook up with the Fraser Lake system. On my next trip this way I would try and blaze the trail over there.

But for now I needed to get going so I moved to pack and hook up the second drag for Lobo. He didn't look all that impressed but he followed behind with his small load like a seasoned sled dog. Reaching the moose meat I realized that with more beaver traps to check I was not going to be able to carry all this home with me. Taking the better part of it to the shore I cut some boughs to pile the meat on and then more to cover it with. That should keep the birds off. Hopefully it would still be there in a few days when I returned.

Arriving where the trail broke off to the west I dropped everything but my axe and disconnected one drag. Checking the sets on Lake 1 and 2 I ended up with a beaver at each house. Pulling the sets out since I had two beavers from each house I worried about the trip home. With about 20 pounds of meat, several marten and four beavers to bring it was quite a load. It had turned into an amazing trip over this trail. Including yesterday this trail had netted me 4 beavers, 5 marten, a mink, a fox and 2 squirrels. Nice!

But now it was another slow and easy trip home. With the two little beavers hooked up for Lobo to pull I had the rest to contend with. Leaning forward to let the weight push me I rested often, as well as having to turn around to unhook Lobos drag from the trees, meant that I made slow progress. But like the night before I pushed onward and knew I would arrive at camp tired but happy. Wish everyday could be like today! I would work that hard for that much reward all day long. The thought of a big moose steak supper pushed me on and within a couple hours I was at camp and ready to eat.

With just the hill now between me and a hot coffee I struggled up, half dragging Lobos beaver along with mine to the top. Dropping everything at the cabins entrance I dug out a good chunk of moose meat for Lobo in thanks for a job well done and went inside. With water on I could hear the chattering of the Whiskey Jacks and Lobos growl as they tried to steal his meat. Crawling back outside with my coffee I set some small pieces of meat on the roof and watched as the birds came floating down from the trees. They grabbed the meat and flew back to stuff it into the crotch of a branch for later use I imagined.

Then I wondered how would I keep my meat fresh and away from the birds at the same time? With a garbage bag laid on a beaver stretcher I placed a layer of meat on it and sprinkled some salt over it, then another bag, more meat and so on. This should freeze and with a second board on top the birds should be kept away. Now however I had a long job ahead of me. I could leave the frozen marten until I got back from Ahmabel Lake but the beavers had to be skinned tonight. If I let them freeze it would take a week to thaw them out.

So with coffee in hand I moved to my skinning area and got started. My Tom Wissel, handmade beaver skinner was sharp and ready to go to work so I jumped right in and with all four skinned in a couple of hours I started the stretching process. By the time I had finished the stretching the squirrels were ready and then I was able to even get the marten done, being careful because there was still some frost in the body. Cool, nothing left to do now but have a coffee and relax before sleep. Tomorrow I was off to Ahmabel Lake. Should my whole bedroll come with me? That decision could be made in the morning.

CANNIBALS

(November 29)

The tree line at the end of Hiawatha Lake grew in the distance as I moved further north. With the eastern sky barely lit up as I made the bush line that led to the Little Fraser River, I was hardly able to see what I was doing as I removed the chunk of frozen bait that had been caught in the trap. There were fresh weasel tracks everywhere and my guess was that he had crawled into the box and tried dragging the bait out with him, springing the trap. Lucky for him the bait was thicker than he was so he was able to escape. I had made an early start this morning because I wanted to have time to re-explore Scuckasu Lake. There had to be a beaver house on that body of water somewhere, and I was intent on finding it.

Gliding along on my snowshoes like a seasoned pro, which at 18 years of age I was fast becoming, I ate up the miles quickly and upon hitting the river I found a marten in the last trap and was met by wolf tracks following my trail. As I proceeded up the trail the wolves (it looked like 6 by the tracks) wandered off, then returned again to follow for awhile longer. The closer I got to the two snares that were set, the more excited I got. They must not have been too hungry though because other than eating one squirrel they didn't bother my traps at all.

Dropping in a snare where ever a spot presented itself I got closer and closer to my sets. With another marten in the trap right before the snares I also left it for the return trip, and hurried to the first snare. But where I had blocked off the trail the wolves had gone off the trail and circled the set about ten feet away. Maybe it didn't look natural enough for them. When they came back on the trail there was now only 4 sets of tracks. Straight down the trail they traveled toward my next snare. Rushing toward the set I saw that the ground was packed down everywhere and there was fur scattered all around. What the...? Are you kidding me? Bending down, I noticed that the fur was from a wolf. You mean that I finally caught a second wolf and his buddies cannibalized him? That sucked! For him and for me!

Finding the drag pole that the snare was attached to I also found the head and a small part of the neck with it. They had eaten almost the entire animal right up to the wire. I was shocked! I had no idea that they would eat one of their own pack members. But maybe this animal was from a different pack of wolves all together. That's it! Now there were going to be snares everywhere. They couldn't eat each other if they were all caught. But seriously, what a piss off!

Fuming I continued on toward Otter lake, and turning north at the lake, made my way to Third Otter. Not paying attention to my surroundings I suddenly noticed where a flock of grouse had dove into the snow. That in itself was not that unusual, but the fact that there were at least 20 holes and none of them had tracks leading away was. I had never seen more than one of these spots at a time before. Walking carefully I got as close as I could before the snow exploded as the birds all took flight. Hey! These were not Ruffed grouse. Now I had never seen one but I had seen pictures and with their telltale flap, flap, flap, glide flying technique they were obviously Sharptail grouse, the bigger cousin to the Spruce and Ruffed grouse that live in the north woods. These were a prairie bird and I wondered what they were doing here? Whatever, it was sure neat to watch at least 20 of them sail away together.

At least it brought my spirits up a little after the wolf debacle. Once they had all disappeared I made my way to my beaver set and with a nice beaver in it I decided to pull the snares. I was really going to have to find some more beaver houses but they could not be grown out of thin air. I could always keep trapping these ones but then there would be absolutely no beavers for next year. My only real option was to get the trail over to Fraser Lake where there should be a few more beaver houses but I was afraid that it was not going to happen till I had a snowmobile out here. The distance was just too great but all this backtracking was just such a waste of time and energy.

Then with an overnight camp on Pody Lake, I would have two circle trails and all the traps could get checked every four or five days. That was going to be in a perfect world, and I was afraid not in this year's plans. Like I said before I think as I walk and all of a sudden I found myself entering the bush on the east end of Otter Lake. With just a mile to Ahmabel Lake and another to the cabin I would have lots of time to head to Scuckasu before dark.

Picking up another marten before I reached the lake I stepped out onto the ice and turned north. As I passed the first little bay I could see that slush had come up and I made a detour around it. Slush is formed when the weight of the snow cracks the ice. The lake water then seeps up through the crack and soaks into the snow. If it soaks all the way to the surface it will freeze rather quickly but if there is snow on top the snow acts as insulation and prevents the slush from freezing. I have seen slush from 4 inches deep to a bad as 18 inches deep on some bigger lakes. It plays havoc on snowmobiles especially if you are pulling a toboggan.

But here my detour didn't work because the snow was so deep in the little bay that I ended up getting into the slush and had to slog my way through a foot of the sloppy mess. With snowshoes that now felt like they weighed a ton, I inched my way to shore. At the shoreline I was in the clear and with the back of my axe head I knocked the slush that had attached itself to my shoes off with a couple good whacks. Again I wondered why God had invented something like slush. There was no real use for it that I could see.

Finally arriving at the camp I dragged the beaver up the hill and noticed a lot of mink tracks around the beaver carcass from the last trip. I guess he was getting a free meal out of me. Inside with a fire going and a pot of snow on the stove, I hung my catch while I waited for the water to boil. Chewing on some beaver jerky I decided that I would make some more with the moose meat also. That should be real good stuff. I had finished off the bannock at Hiawatha, but had brought a bag of the "fixins" with me to cook up here.

Sounds yummy! Moose meat and fresh bannock for supper, what could be better, but for now, a cup of coffee and off again to check a few traps, and maybe explore the rest of Scuckasu Lake? There had to be some beavers somewhere over there. Dragging myself from the warmth of the woodstove, I jumped into my snowshoes and made tracks. This time however I decided to use the ten foot wide trail someone had conveniently put through the bush for me. I mean I could have wandered around the bush for half a day like the last time but hey, I'd already been there and done that!

Cruising up the east shoreline of Scuckasu Lake I passed a group of small islands and then rounded a point just before the river mouth. Here was where the lake drained into the Fraser River so I followed it down to a huge grassy swamp. There, from a distance I spotted a large lump sticking up out of the grass. I knew right off from the size of the "chimney" that this was a live house and a good one at that. But before I set this house up I decided to check the rest of the river. Being that this house was better than two miles from the cabin on Ahmabel it was too far to travel to if it was the only house there. That would be an extra five mile walk to check one beaver house. Not the best use of my time!

This was probably going to have to be done when I had a snowmobile in here. The sun was already getting low in the sky and I hadn't set any traps or checked any for awhile. And that all takes time! Following the river I was careful at any place that looked like it had faster water. The Fraser, when I got to the junction was now quite a large river. Probably fifty feet wide at least, and it was easy travelling. Having to leave the open ice in only a few places because of several rapids I noticed that there was an abundance of fur sign and I was tempted to put traps in. "Not now Dave" I told myself. "Just wait for the snowmobile".

The river mouth was still wide open as I skirted it from inside the bush line. My stomach was in control now and it talked me into walking right past the beaver sets and to check them in the morning. Back at camp I mixed up my bannock mixture with some water and threw it on the stove. As it rose I sipped my coffee and turned it when ready, waiting for that golden brown color. With the bannock cooked I threw in my moose steak after giving Lobo a chunk. He wagged his tail thankfully, knowing he would get his fill once the beaver was skinned. With a dash of salt and pepper my meal was complete, and oh so tasty! Finished with supper I decided to skin the beaver since the rest were still frozen. Twenty minutes later I was tucking the pelt, with the castors rolled up inside, away until the morning.

Out on the porch with a coffee in hand I noticed some movement at the beaver carcass that was left here on my last trip. Standing motionless for a few minutes, sure enough out popped a mink. He looked around and deciding it was safe he crawled up on the beaver and started feeding. That was so cool. There I was standing ten feet from a mink and he either didn't know or didn't care that I was there. I didn't even think of setting a trap for him because I would have enjoyed seeing him whenever I came this way, if he hung around that long.

Deciding that the night was young and I was not ready for sleep yet, I grabbed my pack and my axe and went to check the beaver sets. Lobo just looked at me like I was an idiot when I called him to follow, so I left him in the camp. Down the lake I went, first to the set just around the corner. This spot was sprung so after resetting I crossed the lake and found the trail east to the Fraser River. Finding myself in some slush again I had to clean the shoes off at the edge of the bush before continuing on. It was a little more difficult following the short trail through the bush, but I worked my way through and couple of hours later arrived back at camp, with a beaver and a marten for my troubles.

Perfect! That killed a few hours that I didn't have to spend trying to sleep. Settling in with a coffee I started thinking that right then I was probably closer to HWY #11 to the north than I was to the train tracks to the south. Anyway that was enough thinking, so I curled up in my blanket between the mattresses and went to sleep.

BLIZZARD

(November 30)

Boy the weather can sure change in a hurry. I went to sleep with clear skies and woke up to a howling blizzard. The snow was being blown parallel to the ground by a driving northwest wind that really made it look like my trip home was going to be a little bit uncomfortable. At least my blanket had made sleeping a bit more endurable. But not being in a hurry to venture out into this nightmare, I started skinning the beaver and then slowly packed my gear. The wind was so bad that the cabin would actually shake when a serious gust would assault it. Chewing as slowly as I could through my breakfast I finally had no choice in the matter and with my snowshoes strapped on and my pack slung I was off.

The only good thing was that for a while the wind would be at my back and maybe it would settle down by the time I made it to Otter Lake. Reaching the bush line with just a touch of frost creeping into my right cheek I stopped for a moment to rub it out with my fingers. The next mile was nice as the bush sheltered me from the wind, but stepping out onto Otter Lake I was met by the full force of my first serious Northern Ontario blizzard. With the wind straight into my right eye I made it across the lake but had to stop to pull the ice of my eyelashes because they were frozen shut. I had been in some good storms down south but this was a different sort of deal.

The wind drove the heat from my body and the snow hit me like a million shotgun pellets in a never ending barrage. Now I finally realized why I had not run across any sunbathers on my travels. Once inside the bush I was back into somewhat of a sheltered area. Even when I broke out into the open there was not enough room for the wind to really build since I was heading sort of south west and the bush line was a short distance away. Even so, the sight of Hiawatha Lake was a welcome one until I stepped out and looked south where the lake used to be. Now there was nothing but one wall of swirling snow after the other. I couldn't recall having ever having seen snow blowing in four different directions at the same time before.

The shore line of the lake disappeared less than 100 yards away, but you know I wasn't getting any warmer standing here so I jumped in and made a hole in this mass of snow! A half an hour later I was crawling into the camp door, or should I say I was tunneling down to the door, and inside I was met by a five foot long snow drift inside my cabin. I guess the lack of a proper door was bound to cause some problems at some point. Not like it was overly airtight.

My first order of business was getting a fire going and thankful I was that I knew enough to always have a pile of kindling split for myself. Even with my numb fingers it took but a minute to have the heat radiating from the stove and the water pot on. With not much daylight left and it didn't matter anyway because I was not going back out there for anything, I decided to relax, absorb some warmth and take care of my fur in the morning. Everything, even the skinned beaver pelts were frozen from the trip back. I sat snug and warm in my cabin while Mother Nature pounded the north woods with her fury. Not sure whom she was mad at but something had for sure pissed her off.

With supper done, a coffee in hand and my radio time expired I finally let the warmth take me to dreamland. During the night

I awoke to the sound of nothing. The wind had abated! Good, I would be able to get out in the morning.

(December 1)

BORED!

The wind and snow had picked back up again. I was not going to brave this weather again so I hung around camp, took care of my furs and cut a bunch of firewood. Not an exciting day, but better than freezing out there. Early to bed for a real early start tomorrow!

THOSE WOLVES NEED TO READ THE RULE BOOK

(December 2)

The storm had died off slowly over the afternoon and so my planning for today's travels had begun. Wanting a very early start, to take advantage of every second of daylight, I awoke before any light was in the sky. I was going to make it to Fraser Lake today come hell or high water. I awoke refreshed and eager for the trail, after a whole day being tied up in my cabin. It was still pitch black outside with breakfast done and my bag all packed, so I headed out into the dark. And when I say dark I meant dark! Like pitch black! The thermometer read minus 36 degrees and the air frosted my nostrils as I breathed it in.

My snowshoe trail was invisible from the storm but I could not have followed it anyway. I could barely see my snowshoes on my feet against the white snow. But I figured that by the time I slowly made my way down the lake to my trail it would start to brighten up. My god it was cold, and arriving at the trail head I stopped to wait for some light. Building a fire from the roots of the many blown down trees that lined the shore line I kept warm to a degree that I could handle. I don't know how long I sat there waiting for that sun to show up but at one point I got tired of waiting and walked back to the camp. With still no sign of any light to the east I crawled back into my bed and slept.

When I next awoke there was just a hint of light on the eastern horizon. Well that's the last time I will leave camp before I can see the light starting. Once again I headed out on the trail with Lobo looking at me as if to say "How many times are you going to do this today Dummy". Soon I was in the bush heading toward Chain Lakes. Blaze to blaze I traveled without a hint of a trail in the snow, slogging through the deep snow step after step. The traps were empty other than a squirrel and it seemed that nothing had been moving during the storm. Every box had to be cleaned out as the snow was piled high on top of the traps.

Pulling my otter traps because the creek was frozen right over now, I moved on and just before the moose meat cache I came across wolf tracks. Lots of them in fact and sure enough I followed them right to where I had stored it. Or what used to be my moose meat cache. Now it was just a bunch of spruce boughs scattered around with a little bit of blood on the snow. They had also dug all around the cows head and gnawed it off level with the ice. That was just perfect! Half my meat supply gone but maybe now with this deep snow they would start following my trail more so that my snares would be more effective. Small consolation compared to having my meat all eaten. By Lobo's reaction I guessed that the wolves had just left here not too long ago, he was looking a little spooked.

But why dwell on it? I ain't going to change things by crying in my oatmeal. So I slogged on step after step through the snow. At my turn off point I decided to blaze on the return trip like usual as I followed this very tiny creek. Mainly by staying in the thick Black Spruce stand I followed the drainage until I arrived at the pond which was the end of the system. No beavers! From here it was overland about a mile to the Fraser river headwaters. There were actually two creeks that formed a "V" and I aimed for the middle, not wanting to miss the tiny lake to the north and have a "Scuckasu" incident all over again.

An hour and a half later I noticed a small pond off to my left and drifted over that way. It was not the pond that I was aiming for but the second one down the creek. Perfect! On the way back I would follow the creek back to the pond and then connect with my trail. Really I should have turned around with the trip taking longer than expected with all this snow but the drive to go a little further pushed me on. Another half a mile and I hit the junction of the two creeks. It should only be a mile to the lake but now I really took notice of how far down the sun had dropped in just the last short while.

I was disappointed to have not gotten to Fraser Lake as I turned and double timed it down the trail. I seemed to have forgotten how much fun it was early this morning trying to walk in that pitch blackness. "Ok dog" I said to Lobo. "We had better get a move on before we get into trouble here". As fast as I could move through the bush, we travelled and once into the open area of the lakes we did a jog / run for short spurts not wanting the cold to frost my lungs. But even with that I knew that the dark was going to catch us way short of our goal. Passing the spot where my moose meat had been eaten I observed that the wolves had returned and spent some time scouring the area for more food!

Hurrying past we arrived at Lake 4 in complete darkness, I had to move a lot slower, you know, what with the not being able to see anything and all. Following the trail by feel, if my right snowshoe sank into loose snow I would turn left a bit. Moving like this I finally made it to the trail on Lake 3, where things really got tricky. Once in the bush I literally had to put my hands in front of my face to keep the branches from poking my eyes and to stop me from walking into the trees. What a feeling to look down at white snow and you are not even able to see the snowshoes on your feet.

One step at a time, a tree looms up two feet from your face and your hands reach out to ward off the branches. Your foot sinks so by feel you find the packed trail again. Finally after what seemed like forever I realized that I was in the thick stand of Black Spruce that told me I was about ¾'s of the way to Hiawatha Lake.

Suddenly I heard a low growl coming from Lobo. I turned to him and he crowded right in on my legs. Crouching down I whispered "What is it boy"? A whine was his answer! And then another whine, but not from Lobo this time! This one floated out of the blackness. Wolves! Taking my drag rope from my pocket, I tied it around Lobo's neck. "Easy boy", I crouched there holding him quiet. I could hear the animals footsteps in the snow, they were that close. They would stop and then they would move all in time with our movements. Every time I shifted position they would shuffle around like a well choreographed ballet. There were wolves in front of us, behind us and on both sides of us. Branches scratched as they move through the tight trees rubbing against their fur.

They were circling and I knew they wanted the dog but that wasn't happening that night. Now I knew wolves were supposed to be afraid of people but this bunch was showing a flagrant disregard for that rule. Finally with the wolves not moving off I decided that crouching here was not doing me any good so I stood up and moved off very slowly with Lobo on the leash. Stopping every once in a while I would hear them still following. At one point a branch broke close by and Lobo let out a sharp bark. I gave a yell, taking the bark as a sign that they were possibly getting a little too close for comfort.

Now I know all about Little Red Riding Hood and all those other stories. Fairy tales to be sure but in this blackness and with these wolves all around me, I am not afraid to admit, I was a little spooked! With my axe in one hand and the rope in the other we inched along. Every step was a step closer to getting away from these animals and whether they were curious, wanted the dog or just laughing at me after eating all my moose meat, I didn't care. I just knew that they were to close for my liking. Finally after what seemed like an eternity my snowshoes started pointing downhill and I knew we were but a hundred yards or so from the lake. At this point Lobo stopped his mix of whining and growling and I took that to mean that the wolves had left for parts unknown.

The bush parted and we were finally on the lake. The darkness that covered the lake now seemed like bright daylight compared to that black hole we had just crawled through. Now, with the wolves nothing but a memory, all I wanted was some food and a hot coffee. I decided then and there to go back there in the morning to check the tracks and see what I could decipher about the evenings events. Besides I had not been able to check all of my traps today.

At last, at who knew what time, I trudged up the hill to the cabin. I tossed Lobo a good chunk of beaver meat and got busy making supper while waiting for the coffee water to boil. Scraping the last bit of jam from the jar I spread it ever so lovingly on a chunk of bannock and with coffee in hand enjoy the first bite I'd had in probably 14 hours. Gosh that was delicious!

At least the heavy snowshoeing had kept me warm in this bitter cold. The thermometer read -20 degrees. It had warmed up a little since this morning. Now after what seemed like the longest day of my life, although kind of an exciting one, I crawled into bed and slept like the dead.

(December 3)

Over breakfast I discovered that I had made a mistake the day before. The spot that I had turned around was not the creek junction that I had been looking for. It was actually a small creek that was not even on the map. And to top it off the junction that I was looking for did not even exist. The two streams actually both flowed into Fraser Lake only about 100 yards apart. I had turned around less than a mile from the lake. Well I was heading back in that direction mainly to make sure all the traps were in working order but I really wanted to go and read the sign left by the wolves. I was curious to see how really close they had been to Lobo and I.

The trip to Pody Lake could wait a day, and I was thinking that I may have to break that trip into two days, with the depth of this snow. I didn't mind walking 10 to 15 miles in a day but not breaking trail through that deep of snow the whole way. But for now I would finish my coffee, continue salting and hanging some moose meat to dry and relaxing a bit before my days adventure. Finally ready Lobo and I took off and once on the lake Lobo decided to try walking on the back end of my snowshoes again. The first time I just gave him a look but on his second attempt he got a blast and that was it. He pulled a 180 and with the old "tail between the legs and I'm not listening to you" run, he booted it all the way back to camp. Whatever dog! Go ahead sleep it off, I'll be fine. You have four legs I've only got two. But don't worry about me. And he didn't!

On I travelled, stopping only to clear my fox set and a mink set. Reaching the top of the hill I discovered that the wolves had indeed followed us right to the hill. There had been seven wolves in the pack and following the trail I was able to put a picture together of what had went on less than ten hours ago. I could see plainly where the animals had circled in front of us because my tracks crossed over theirs and where they had circled behind their tracks were on top of mine. Where we had stopped and first heard them they had actually been less than 10 feet from us and at one point only 7 feet. That made the hair on the back of my neck bristle again.

That close and I had not been able to see a thing! From that point on they had followed right behind us on the trail, never leaving it until I got to the spot where they had stolen my moose meat. Here it looked like they had just hidden in the bush till we went by and then decided to come and check us out. At that point I was thinking maybe it was good that they had eaten all my moose meat. What might have happened if they had been hungry? Might they have been more inclined to press a little harder to get at Lobo? So maybe that moose dying like that after all was a godsend to me. Who knows? But it was for sure interesting to study the wolf's actions, and it gave me a little more insight into their behavior patterns.

Progressing down the trail I reached Lake 8 with nothing to show for the day so I decided to proceed to Lake 9 and across the trail over to Little Fraser River. That would partially break my trail to Ahmabel Lake plus give me a nice circle trail. Arriving at Hiawatha Lake a couple of hours later I looked out over the lake at the mass of huge snow drifts. It was a sight to see for sure and stepping out I discovered that for the most part the wind had packed the snow so tight it was actually nice walking in most places.

At the mouth of the narrows I got into slush big time. Here the snow had really piled up and I guess the weight of it had cracked the ice and created the slush. It was so bad that I thought it was going to be over my boots. What a horrible time trying to walk through this slop all the way to shore. Finally I made it but my snowshoes were all weighted down again. Removing the slush with several whacks from my axe I continued on to camp. Skunked for the day but happy that all my sets were again in working order I climbed the hill and gave Lobo a sideways glance. He discreetly avoided my eyes and acted like I had never even left.

With supper finished and coffee in hand I went outside and stood in the dim light that eased through the cabin "door". Off to the southeast I could hear wolves howling. Was it the same bunch from last night? I tried to distinguish between the different animals but they were too far away to really tell. The sorrowful sound carried to me and I let out with an imitation call as best I could. The howl would start off low and then build in volume till it ended abruptly. The animals went silent for a minute and I continued with my calling. In no time they started up again and sure enough Lobo decided to join in. It was a musical interlude that I would never forget.

Finally after awhile, the wolves were finished and Lobo and I crawled back inside. The outside noises gave way to the sound of firewood crackling in the stove and water boiling in the kettle. Before bed I decided to take stock of my food supply. It looked like with my moose meat I should have enough flour, oatmeal and cornmeal but my coffee, sugar and tea were going to be touch and go but if I conserved it I should be ok until the plane came in. I guess I could always eat the dog. Ya, I'm kidding! WINK-WINK! Well off to bed. Tomorrow would be another long day.

(December 4)

Still cold the next morning! Minus 32, but at least there was not even the slightest breeze blowing so the cold did not feel so bad. I tried a breakfast of tea and oatmeal this morning. Not my favorite by any means but at least it filled the hole and would help stretch out my rations. Chewing on a little moose jerky I loaded up my pack for the trip to Pody Lake. In the first trap right behind camp I found a marten and as I was swapping out the frozen animal for a new trap Lobo gave it a sniff. "Cool, hey dog", I said, and he wagged his tail in response. I guessed his mood was over and he was going to grace me with his presence today.

At set # 2 the wolf trap was completely covered so I reset it and noticed marten tracks under the box. The same went for several of the sets as I traveled along the trail. The animals had really been moving over night but with the traps all snowed in they wouldn't or couldn't push their way through the snow. Finally at the first set on the west shoreline of Pody Lake I caught my second marten of the day. Trudging my way up the lake I picked up a beaver in the snare set at the north end of Pody. A beaver that was very much needed for bait I might add. But at least with the moose meat at home I could use the entire beaver for bait instead of eating some of it. I normally got between 10 and 18 pieces of bait off each beaver carcass depending on the size, but between the bait being stolen and feeding Lobo it seems to disappear faster than I could catch it.

Now it was decision time! Do I break trail all the way around to Little Pody or spend a little time and set the east creek beaver house? If I checked Little Pody I could leave for Ahmabel a day earlier, but I may not get back till after dark again. And with these temperatures did I really want to sleep in the Ahmabel cabin? NOT!!!

So it was the east creek that won out. I headed that way, dragging my beaver along behind me. Arriving at the lodge just a quarter mile from the lake I dropped in a snare set and seeing the telltale sunken snow near the house I cleared an area for a very well used entrance set. Wanting to see what was up this creek further I started pushing north. For an hour I walked through the crotch deep snow, one dead beaver pond after another until finally reaching the end of the long narrow lake I turned around disappointed. But at least the walk back would be easier now with the trail broken.

Stopping only long enough to shoulder my dragline, I continued south down the lake. Arriving at the junction of the trail to the east, I again had to talk myself out of breaking the rest of the trail to Little Pody but common sense and a deep desire to not have to walk home in the pitch black again won over and I turned east along the broken trail. Lobo and I enjoyed a leisurely walk through the bush and made it back to camp well before sunset. So that is what my cabin looked like in the daylight!

Hanging my catch I prepared an early supper of moose meat and bannock. The heat from the stove felt really nice as I ate and sipped on my coffee. Finished I talked myself into cutting some firewood till the darkness arrived. You could never have too much firewood as I had come to realize. This weather burnt through the wood at an alarming pace. At dark I crawled back inside and got to the skinning. The beaver was first since it was the only thawed animal and an hour later it was clean skinned and stretched into a perfect extra-large oval.

My fur pile was getting fairly large but I was really wishing that I had more beaver houses to set. It seemed that with every trip I was pulling beaver sets out because I had caught enough from that colony. At some point I was going to run out of houses to set. This was really quite a difference from down south where I had been trapping. With the entire bush down there being poplar with the odd White pine thrown in the beavers were far more abundant than they were in this mainly over mature coniferous forest. Great bush for martens but not so much for beavers it would seem. Several of the houses that looked like they had a large number of beavers in them I had already cheated and taken three animals from them. The recommended number is two per colony, like with marten the number is three males for every female you catch. When you get close to one to one you start depleting your breeding stock. I have read that with muskrats a person can harvest up to 80 % of the population without hurting it. They can have several litters a year if the food is there so they will replenish the supply. It would sure be nice if the marten did that.

For now I would have to conserve my beaver population and keep my harvest to a minimum. Having found only 20 live houses so far I was not overly optimistic that the unexplored portion of my trap line was going to be crawling with the giant rodents.

With a cup of tea and some music, I jotted down some notes in my journal and it was lights out.

(December 5)

My first order of business the next morning was to skin yesterdays marten catch. They should be ready to flip by the time I got home from the Little Pody Lake trail. With that chore done I mixed up a batch of cornmeal pancakes. They were barely edible with jam on them, and while scraping the very last drops out of the jar, I knew they were not going to taste any better after today. But it was food and I did have to admit, it was better than nothing.

The morning passed on the trail to Little Pody, and arriving there with 3 squirrels and a marten I decided to go and check out the creek mouth where the otters had travelled to. It was just a short walk and of course Lobo decided to stay and "guard" the pack. I called it being lazy but I guess he figured that it needed guarding with all that valuable fur in it. Once at the creek I found myself in a virtual (not virtual by today's standards) otter playground. Small rapids through narrow rock walls and nice smooth rock faces covered in snow with otter sign everywhere. Open water at the bottom of the rapids where the otters had been climbing out of the ice, made for promising looking set locations. But without any traps with me it would have to wait.

Out of curiosity I followed the creek until it opened up on a large bay at the north end of Nagagami Lake. At this point I realized that I had crossed my trap line boundary so I turned around and booted her back to my pack and the lazy dog. Loading the pack and with Lobo falling in behind me we hit the end of Little Pody and upon reaching the beaver house between the two lakes I picked a nice beaver out of the snares. There was a mink hanging in a marten set within sight of the lodge also. This trip was turning out to be pretty good so far. Pretty close to every trap had either an animal in it, or it was sprung or at least has some fresh tracks close by.

Finally reaching Pody Lake I kept an eye out for a good spot for a fox snare set. Thick willows would be perfect but even a thick stand of small Spruce would do fine. Locating a spot just up the east shore a ways I wired a chunk of beaver to a small tree and then snow shoed three trails out to the lake in a "V" pattern. Placing an 8 inch snare on each trail about a foot off the ground I was finished in short order.

Minutes later I was on the hard packed trail from the day before and moving along quickly. Funny though, I had not seen a wolf track all day, and that hadn't happened very often out here. In the last few traps that I had checked yesterday I caught just one weasel. They sure were cute little guys and probably only worth a couple of bucks, but if he was nice enough to jump into my trap I would be nice enough not to waste him.

With the sun behind the trees we arrived back at camp, wore out from the long trip. Tomorrow was going to be a killer trip for sure and I was happy that I had broken part of the trail the other day even if it was only a couple of miles, it was at least a start! Inside the camp I relaxed over a coffee and hung my fur to dry and thaw. I knew that I should be drinking tea in the evenings but I really needed a coffee bad. Tea would do for the rest of the night.

It was cornbread and moose meat for supper and while I was at it I threw Lobo a chunk. He seemed to appreciate it and I figured that there was enough for a couple of weeks, and that should bring me close to the pickup day. An hour later with the beaver skinned and stretched I tackled the squirrels. A half an hour later the marten and mink were still frozen and would have to wait till morning to be skinned. Fixing up an experimental bait set for otters was my last chore of the evening before crawling into bed. I had taken my eight inch Rapala fishing lure out of my tackle box and removed the hooks. I then attached it to the trigger of a 330 conibear trap to set under the ice. I knew the perfect place to make this set tomorrow on my way to Ahmabel.

Right now though sleep was needed bad so without even bothering to turn on the radio I stoked the fire and hit the bed. Dead to the world in seconds, I was!

BACK TO AHMABEL AND
AN AMAZING SIGHT

(December 6)

In the morning with breakfast finished and my animals taken care of I hovered over my second cup of coffee. Knowing that the trip to Ahmabel Lake was going to be a long arduous trek I gulped the last mouthful and crawled out of the camp. Nice! The temperature had warmed up some to the 5 degree mark. Perfect walking and with a gorgeous clear blue sky it was good that I would be walking north this morning. The bright sunlight was horrible to walk into for long periods, and with the light reflecting off the snow it would almost blind me after a few hours. I would end up walking with my hat pulled over my eyes or holding my hand up to shield them from the sun. I remembered the book from school called "Lost in the Barrens" by Farley Mowat and how he had described the phenomena called snow blindness. To this day my eyes are still super sensitive to bright light.

With my pack loaded with everything needed for this trip I shouldered the load and started down the hill. Once on the lake I noticed that there was a good breeze blowing that had not been noticeable in the bush. That was perfect as it would keep me cool while walking. One other bonus about the wind was that it would pack the snow on the lake even harder and make for easier snowshoeing. An hour later I was on the Little Fraser River with a squirrel and a marten in the first two traps. There were fresh tracks at both boxes, which was always a good sign, so maybe they would in the sets on the way back.

As I progressed along the river most of the traps were sprung and the bait gone. It looked like the heavy snow had slowed the traps down enough that the animals missed getting caught. Finally snagging another one between Otter and Second Otter Lakes I carried on to the beaver set and was rewarded with a small beaver. Backtracking to Otter Lake I moved east along the Ahmabel trail and found a bunch of otter sign at the next beaver house. They had chewed their way through the dam and the rushing water had worked a hole through the ice below the dam. There I found again more blood and a couple fish scales. This was the perfect spot for my new otter trap. Sliding a dead pole through both springs I wired it solid and then cut a hole in the ice right beside where the otters had slipped into the water. Attaching a cross pole made the set complete.

With nothing in the beaver set I decided to bring fresh bait with me on the return trip. Down the trail a ways I couldn't believe how deep the snow was. That huge log that I had been crawling over every trip was now completely buried in the snow. The one big branch that I walked under before was now in my way and I had to duck under it to get by. I tried breaking it off but being about three inches thick, it took all my weight to bend it right down to the snow but it still would not break. On the way back tomorrow I would carry my axe out of the pack and cut it off. Right now I was in a hurry!

Nothing at all was in the rest of my traps and as I arrived at the cabin I noticed that my pack was sure light. I had used up every bit of bait that I had brought along. Lucky I had caught that small beaver because the wolves had been to the camp also. The beaver carcasses that I had left there were completely gone. Dropping everything in the camp I started a fire, put on a pot of snow to melt and taking just my pack and axe I rushed to get to the last two beaver traps before dark.

I left Lobo in the camp, because for the last couple of miles the snow had been balling up between his toes pretty bad. Several times we had to stop, so he could chew the snowballs of his feet. He deserved a rest anyway so I took off for the traps alone. Heading up the river trail first it was good to see a marten hanging at the set just off the lake shore. At the beaver house I took off my snowshoes and using one as a shovel I cleared all the snow from over the hole and got to chopping. A nice beaver was my reward for the effort and slipping my shoes back on I headed back to camp. The camp beaver set would get checked in the morning. I was just too tired from the walk, and really didn't want to chop another hole through the ice tonight.

Back in the cabin, some more snow was added to the pot and I decided to cut some firewood to start replacing the wood that had been burnt so far this winter. For now though I needed to eat some food, drink a cup of tea, and do a little relaxing by the wood stove before I cut wood and skinned some beavers. They were still a little wet after supper but I could deal with that when I got back to Hiawatha so first I cut the feet off and tossed them to Lobo, they were his favorite, I think they were like candy to him. He always ate the front feet first then the back feet and then the tail. Always in that exact order!

Finally supper finished and with the beavers skinned and the castors cut out and rolled up in the hides I rolled myself up in my blanket and crawled between the mattresses. The firewood would have to wait until morning now. As I relaxed I thought back on some of the crazy stuff that had happened to me since I had landed. Then I wondered again how Bill and Don were doing on their trap lines. Sleep eventually grabbed a hold of me and I didn't stir till the cold drove me from my bed to add wood to the stove. Several times during the course of the night I woke, shivering violently, until the sun finally poked its warming face over the tree line.

(December 7)

Looking out the window of the Ahmabel camp I saw the sky turning a bright pink as the sun tried to push its way higher and higher over the horizon. Red sky at night, sailors delight, red sky in morning, sailors take warning. The old saying made me wonder what was going to happen today, weather wise. Whatever it was it was not going to change my plans at all. I still had to check the last beaver trap around the corner, cut some wood and then hoof it back to Hiawatha Lake. But first things first! I needed a coffee, but was going to settle for a hot tea. A very poor substitute in my opinion but with some imagination on my part it was as good as coffee. Ya right! Anyway I decided to check the beaver trap before I ate breakfast, so with my tea done I strapped on my shoes and set out with axe in hand.

Leaving Lobo in camp since the walk home would be far enough I rounded the point just north of the cabin and was treated to the most amazing site. Just past the beaver house there was a steady stream of birds flying west to east across the lake. From their flight patterns I could tell that they were those Sharptail grouse that I had first seen at Otter Lake. I was not sure how many had already crossed the lake but as I walked toward them I started counting. By the time I reached the spot that they were flying from I had counted 127 grouse that had flown across Ahmabel Lake. And they were still coming! From the lake I could see dozens and dozens of the big birds perched in the trees. Some trees had so many birds that they were bent over right to the ground from the weight of them.

It was hard to count how many birds there were there because they kept flying from one tree to the next. Then one would take off across the lake and several others would follow. More would land from farther out in the bush but the closest I could figure was that there were at least 200 of these big grouse still on the shore. That means well over three hundred grouse in one flock. And me with no gun!!!! Now remember that the sharptails that I had run into about a week ago were the first that I had ever seen. Since that day, trapping in the same basic region for the next 25 years I never saw another Sharptail grouse.

Even the last ten years trapping in Manitoba I have only seen two Shaprtails in the forested area. There are a lot, of course out in the farm land, but they are a prairie bird so that is where a person would expect to see them. All in all it was one of the coolest things I had ever witnessed, just like the caribou migration. If caribous could fly, weighed about three pounds and there was only 350 in a herd. But since I had never seen that, this was the coolest!

After watching for awhile I needed to get going so turning around I went to check the beaver set. One more beaver meant another house to pull the traps from. Boy was I running out of beaver houses fast. Back at the cabin I did a quick breakfast, a quicker skinning job on the beaver and then loaded up for the trip home. The firewood was going to have to wait, again!

Lobo seemed happy to be heading home also and the trip passed by rather uneventfully until I picked up a weasel in a mink cubby and a squirrel in a marten box between Little Fraser River and Hiawatha Lake. Finally out on the lake I ate up the couple of miles to the camp and rounding the last point I was surprised by the sight of three wolves trotting down the shoreline in a southerly direction. It looked like two adults and one pup, and the pup seemed to be having a good time. It would jump around and nip at the bigger animals and they just ignored it as they continued on their way.

Cool to see and it could only have been better if I had my gun with me. Watching until they disappeared from view I moved toward the camp. Surprised, I noticed that their tracks had come right down my trail from the cabin! I did not have a good feeling as I climbed the hill and cresting it my fears were confirmed. They had gotten into my moose meat supply and it was completely gone. Studying the sign I saw that they had come right down my trail from Pody Lake way.

Now instead of pissed, I was excited again. I had a wolf trap under the marten box just a half mile away from here. Crawling into the camp I started a fire and then could stand it no longer. I grabbed the 22 and took off to check the wolf trap. Getting close I could see that the whole area was trampled down. Looking, but finding no trail where a wolf had dragged the drag pole away I started digging around in the snow. Right away I started finding clues. Clues in the form of trap parts. The wolf had literally twisted so hard it had popped the trap jaws right out of the base and the parts were all just lying in a two foot circle. Why I had set one of my oldest traps for wolves I'll never know but I chalked it up to a learning curve. And these darn wolves were the teachers! I figured that because the drag was frozen to the ground the wolf had been able to exert such pressure on the old trap that the steel just bent under the strength of the animal.

Now, I was deeply disappointed, and at the same time utterly amazed at the strength of these animals. Once again I had been bested by these critters. The score now was wolves three, Dave one. But the game was far from over. On the way back to camp I chopped down a firewood tree and carried it with me. Stopping for a second, I readied a snare set so that in the morning I would just have to drop in the snare and it would be good to go.

Once inside the cabin I made myself a coffee and hung my furs to dry before stretching them. Outside I could hear my whiskey jack buddies cackling up a storm. I guessed that Lobo was keeping them off the bait pile or what was left of it after the wolves and they were none too happy about it. By the time my supper was finished the sun had gone down and it was time to take care of my furs.

With everything done I stretched out and listened to the radio for awhile before bed. Going through my food supply now that the moose meat was all gone I came to the conclusion that I was going to get hungry before the plane came in to get me. I would try carrying my gun with me but the trips were so long now that the extra few pounds really put a drag on me. Anyway a few lines in the journal and I was off to dreamland.

(December 8)

The Pody Lake trail was quiet on this particular morning. With breakfast done and my fur waiting for my return I had taken off, and now almost at Pody Lake I had nothing to show for it. The only thing in the traps had been a flying squirrel. At the lake I turned north toward the creek where I had made the beaver sets on the last trip here. As I approached the pond I kept my eyes open for a nice Poplar bait tree and finding one I brought it with me for spare bait. Lucky too, because the snare set was sprung and the bait gone. Resetting it, I next checked the entrance set and picked up a small beaver.

Back on Pody I headed for the beaver house at the north end of the lake and there I had a nice big beaver. Pulling the traps out I also collected the marten set that was in behind the beaver house. It was too far to walk to just check a single marten trap and it would not be very good use of my limited time. Now though I had a small beaver in my pack and a big one on the dragline. And still another set to check between the two Podies! Being at this point almost 10 miles from the camp I decided that I had better shift gears.

Knowing that I was going to arrive home after dark for sure, I was at least happy that there would be a little moonlight tonight to guide my way. And I had not seen any fresh wolf tracks to worry about. Pointing my face south I followed it at a good pace until I hit the end of the lake. Stopping for just a minute to clear the snow from my fox set I hurried down the river. Finally I picked up a marten in one of the pole sets and another beaver at the house. This one was for Lobo to pull and again he didn't look to happy about being put to work. But with his help we should get home a little sooner.

Little Pody came into sight and with it the home stretch. Picking up another marten and a squirrel I reached the cabin about an hour after dark. Lobo looked beat and I knew it was harder for him to pull being lower to the ground than me, but you know what, "you have four legs and I just have two. So suck it up buddy! Besides you haven't had to save my life in almost a month now". And I had already paid him back for that by not letting the wolves eat him the other night.

With a hot tea right away I delayed supper till some of the skinning was done. Then with a full belly I worked late into the night skinning and stretching the catch from today. The martens had to wait till morning when they would be thawed. At last I turned on some music and relaxed. Soon I was asleep and the radio turned itself off as the batteries finally gave up the ghost. I never moved a muscle till morning rolled me out of bed.

FOOD IS IN SHORT SUPPLY

(December 9)

Changing things up a little this morning I made bannock with a mixture of flour and corn meal. It looked like I had enough flour for about a week before I would run out. With no jam left and my sugar all but gone I decided to save the sugar for putting on my oatmeal. I could drink sugarless coffee but that oatmeal was horrible with nothing added. No matter what I did there was going to be a few days where my meals were going to be very plain indeed.

I decided that I had better start carrying my gun again, to try and pick up some grouse. Even though I had not seen one in awhile other than the huge flock by Ahmabel. Not sure how long it would last, because carrying that extra few pounds in my hands wore me out. I would try strapping it across my pack and hopefully that would be easier. My guess was that with no rabbits anywhere near here, the fox and marten were hitting the grouse population pretty hard. Not to mention all the birds I had shot earlier.

With my bannock finished I saved some and mixed up a small amount of oatmeal. That and coffee was my breakfast. At least my coffee looked like it would last till the pickup day. That was good because I really didn't want to think about not having any coffee.

Finally I gathered my gear and made my way down the lake and on to the Chain Lake trail. At my fox snare set the wind had blown the snow in and covered the snares. A fox had walked right down the one trail and stepped right over the snare. Darn! But once in the bush I had better luck, picking up a marten and a squirrel before I hit Lake 3. My wolf snares were not touched and come to think of it I hadn't seen a fresh wolf track all day so far. Moving north I picked up another marten between Lakes 4 and 5 and a beaver at Lake 8.

Now do I pull this house or take another beaver? Finally deciding that I had already taken extra beavers from too many houses, I opted to pull the sets. With one more marten on the trail between Chain Lakes and the Little Fraser river today's catch had turned out to be quite good. Once on the river I saw where a few otters had slid down the ice and buried under the snow. From there they must have gotten into the water somehow and that was good. They were headed in the direction of my new otter set.

Back on track I added two squirrels and a weasel to my pack by the time I hit Hiawatha Lake, looked like I would be busy skinning tonight. As I was snowshoeing down the lake I glanced to my right, and there on the shore, were three moose browsing on the balsam trees. Why they were eating those things I would never understand, but they must get something out of it. I wondered if I could get close enough to put a 22 shot right behind the ear of one of the moose. Would that kill it? It would sure solve my whole food shortage problem, but there was no way I could talk myself into taking the chance of wounding one of those animals and having it wander off somewhere to die.

So licking my lips, I moved on south and left several hundred pounds of fresh meat standing there staring at me. Back at camp, with a cup of tea in hand I again thought of those moose. Boy, a thick juicy moose steak would sure taste great right now. But at least I had a beaver that I could eat some of the meat from.

I figured I had better get skinning the fur and so got started on the beaver. The fur was still a little wet but by lifting the skin up on the nails it would be ok with some air flow between the fur and the board. Once it was skinned, I removed the fat for my lamps and the back legs for food. The rest went for bait which I was plenty short of also. Deboning one of the legs I rolled it in cornmeal and I fried it up nice and crispy. With some warmed up bannock it made an edible meal. Well, edible by my standards anyway, but remember, I ate pancakes with mouse terds in them.

Soon all the animals that were thawed were skinned and stretched and it was time for some rest. Tomorrow was going to be another long day. With the sounds of Kapuskasing radio playing in my ears I wondered to myself where the rest of the animals of the north were hiding. I didn't think I was far enough north to encounter wolverines, but the rest of them like lynx and fishers should be around. But I guessed with no rabbits the lynx would starve anyway, and come to think of it, I had not seen a porcupine or even a track of one since I had arrived either. Maybe that's why there were no fishers? But more likely it was also the lack of rabbits.

TWO WEEKS UNTIL PICKUP

(December 10)

As I awoke I realized that it was now only two weeks before the plane was coming to get me. I was starting to look forward to having some real good food to eat. And a nice cold bottle of coke! Filling my belly with bannock and oatmeal, I washed it all down with a couple cups of hot coffee. I was drinking it black since I had decided to save the precious sweetener for the morning oatmeal.

Planning on carrying my gun with me just in case I saw some grouse again, I packed my gear for the trip and started out. "Ready to go there, Lobo" I asked as he finished off the last of the dry dogwood that I had poured out for him. I knew he would rather have had some beaver meat but I needed that for bait so dry dog food it was. Finally we were on our way, so I had my snowshoes pointed north and I followed them all the way to the end of the lake.

Having picked up nothing at all before I reached the Little Fraser River, on and on I travelled checking each box for bait as I went. Arriving at Otter Lake with only a squirrel to show for my effort I was a little disappointed with the production. But at the next beaver house I had a real nice beaver and checking my otter set was very happy to pull out a big dog otter. My lure set had worked! I was going to have to get some more fish shaped attractants out there.

Once I came to the big log I decided that I was going to cut that branch out of there. I tossed down the pack and pulled the axe out. Taking a couple swings at the big branch was a waste of time. It just vibrated and the axe hardly made a mark in it. So grabbing it by the end I forced it all the way down and holding it with my left hand I lifted my axe to cut it right at the snow level. Suddenly the end of the branch that I had been holding broke off in my hand and the rest of it came up and caught me right in the mouth. The force was enough to make me do a somersault backwards into the snow. Shaking my head I sat up and of course looked around to make sure no one had seen that stupid move.

Boy what a wallop though! My mouth was cut on the inside in four places and on the outside in three. One of my teeth was broken and another was loose. But I guess if I could take that punch, I didn't have to worry about any bar fights bothering me. Getting to my feet I dug down into the snow to the base of the branch and with a few swings of the axe the branch was done. Probably should have done that in the first place. Ya, my hindsight is pretty good. Finished, I reloaded my pack and the beaver drag and moved out. As I walked I could feel my face starting to swell up already. But it reminded me that even a simple thing like cutting a branch could turn into a serious problem out here.

Finally at the Ahmabel camp it was like the marten had fallen off the face of the earth. I had seen the odd track but not enough to get excited about. Not even any wolf tracks in that whole distance. With enough daylight left I decided to check the remaining traps so I could get an early start in the morning. One more small beaver and a marten finally in the trap on the east side of Ahmabel Lake. But this beaver was enough out of this set and now I had only one beaver set on this whole trail. I could always go and set the house on Scuckasu Creek but that meant having to spend an extra night here every trip. I decided that it could wait till I came back with a snowmobile.

I was not sure where all those grouse had gone but my rifle was feeling heavy and without any grouse around I was not going to be carrying it again. Back at camp, with a nice fire going and a hot cup of tea in my hands, I hung the beavers to dry. Luckily the weather was still fairly warm out so the cabin warmed enough that the otter was able to dry even away from the stove. When the first beaver had dried good enough, I skinned it out and gave Lobo a good chunk of meat for his supper. Cutting some off for myself I cut the rest into bait sized pieces and then started on number two. The dry fur I left in the pack to stay frozen till we got back to Hiawatha the next day.

The otter dried off nicely so I rough skinned it and stowed it away with the beaver hides. The second beaver carcass went outside and I covered it with firewood to keep all the ravens off. The Whiskey jacks could still get their little heads in there to eat a bit but I didn't mind that since they were too small to eat much of it. One more cup of tea and I got myself settled between the mattresses. Boy did I need another good sleeping bag!

(December 11)

Well, in the morning I made an executive decision. I was not going to spend another night in this camp without a sleeping bag. The temperature had dropped during the night and I spent the night flipping like a pig on a spit trying to stay warm. I would pull all the traps out east of the beaver house just between Otter and Ahmabel Lakes. That would give me a 7-8 mile trip one way and I thought a 15 mile return trip would be doable in a day. Considering there were very few beaver sets anymore, which meant less ice chopping. It might be a little tight for daylight, but it was not like I was not already getting home after dark fairly regular anyway.

I would be back to reset this area after Christmas when I hopefully would have a snowmobile to get around on. With the decision made I hurried through breakfast and rushed off to pull the marten sets. An hour later I was heading south with my pack fully loaded, pulling traps as I went. Leaving the beaver and otter sets in, I added another marten set near the house since this was as far as I was going to be travelling each trip.

Boy the temperature had really dropped because this cold was biting into my face whenever I got into an open area. The wind caused my eyes to water and while crossing Otter Lake my right eye froze shut again. But soon enough I was off the lake and back behind the sheltering bush. Just past the lake I caught a nice marten in the first set but then there was nothing. Mile after mile I travelled with not a track, without a single animal in all the traps. The only life I saw was one of my old friends the Great Grey owl. He or she sat atop its perch as I traveled past, its head rotating on top of its body, following my progress until I disappeared around a bend in the river.

I guess that owl and I were the only things stupid enough to be out here on this cold day. Finally back on Hiawatha Lake I was down to the home stretch, and the wind was no longer in my eyes but was hitting the back side of my head. Collar up and hat pulled down I arrived at the camp with just a touch of frostbite on my right ear.

Getting a fire going I noticed that my stalactite and corresponding ice flow had expanded with no fire to keep them in check. With bannock, oatmeal and some beaver for supper, I splurged and had a nice cup of coffee with it. Gosh was I ever getting sick of that oatmeal!

I had been checking my fish lines everyday with nothing to show for it so I decided to try jigging for awhile. A half an hour later I gave up on that idea and went to cut some firewood before night set in. Back in the camp, I checked the fur and since the animals were not going to be thawed till the morning, I fiddled around with my snowshoes, replacing a length of the lamp wick that was close to wearing through.

Checking on my food again, hoping that I had missed something (I hadn't), I again realized that I would be completely out of most everything other that my favorite oatmeal in a week. With my bait needed, I poured Lobo a pile of his dry dog food and looking at it I thought "what the heck" and popped a nugget in my mouth. Hmmm tastes like chicken! Actually I didn't think it was all that bad. But for now I would stick with the human food even though the dog food tasted better than oatmeal.

Deciding to stay at camp the next day to stock up on fire wood I finally kicked back and with a cup of tea listened to some Kapuskasing radio. Boy would a can of Coke and a Mars bar go over good right now I thought to myself. It was unreal how much I craved anything sweet. I had not had any substantial sugar for weeks now. And for a guy that would normally drink several pop a day and had a terrible sweet tooth that was saying a lot.

(December 12)

Waking late I sipped on my coffee and filled my belly. Cornmeal cakes made with the last of my cornmeal. I'll tell you what. Anyone who wants to go on a diet I can recommend one, oatmeal, cornmeal, bannock and the occasional bit of meat. Add in snowshoeing 8-15 miles a day with a good load on your back and in no time there will not be an ounce of fat on you.

Getting started on my fur was the first order of business. While I was skinning the marten that I caught on the jump over toward East Ahmabel, something weird happened. I was pulling the hide past the front legs and then over the neck when the entire pelt tore in half. I was like, "what the heck, I'm not that strong". The pelt was torn in a perfectly straight line. Upon closer inspection

I felt a piece of wire along the line where the fur had separated. It was rabbit snare wire! The marten had got its self caught in a rabbit snare, broke the wire and travelled at least to my best guess 15 to 20 miles to get into my marten set. Unless there was someone trapping closer than that and I had no idea about? But with my sewing kit I sewed the two halves together and I did such a good job that the pelt was not even graded damaged.

By that time the sun had warmed the air a little bit and I was ready to go out and cut some firewood. Green birch was still plentiful and the dry wood was too. But the dry wood was getting further to carry every day. It would sure be nice when I had a snowmobile and a sleigh to drag wood with. Not to mention a chainsaw for cutting! It was scary how fast the wood disappeared in this real cold weather, and we had not even reached the coldest months yet.

It would not be a good thing to get hurt out here and not have enough wood to last until the plane came to get me. By the time I had been working at it for several hours the woodpile was at a respectable level. I figured it should be enough for a few weeks at least. Finally before dark I went and checked my camp set. Nothing, but the mice and squirrels had been eating the bait and it needed to be replaced. But it would wait till tomorrow.

Now was the time for breakfast or was it supper? The food is all the same no matter what meal it is. Cup of tea in hand I relaxed in bed and listened to the radio. Making a few notes before I closed my eyes for the night I wondered again how the guys were doing back in White River. Probably sitting in the bar right now having a beer after a big juicy steak dinner. Ahhh crap, I'm going to sleep.

SOMETIME DURING THE NIGHT

(December 13)

My eyes snapped open! Not quite sure what had woke me up but then a growl from Lobo let me know. Funny though, he had not done that in awhile but then the reason became clear. Wolves! And they were real close! Grabbing my coat, slipping on my boots and with rifle in hand I snuck down to the lake shore. There in the moonlight about halfway to the point I could see them. Through the scope I saw three wolves standing facing me, probably wondering what I was. Resting the gun against a tree I kept my crosshairs on one, waiting for it to turn broadside. About 200 yards out I was figuring should be a dead center shot. I just wanted a bigger target. Finally as if on cue they turned to the north and I let loose on my victim. Watching it go down I cranked the bolt and slid another bullet into the chamber. With the gun emptied on the high speed animals I looked back to check on the one that I had shot, just in time to watch it hobble toward the bush. Wishing I had thought to bring extra bullets I just watched as it made the bush line and disappeared.

Tracking it in the morning seemed like a better plan than going off half cocked following a wounded wolf in the darkness. Checking the moon I realized that there was still a lot of night left so I made my way up the hill and crawled back into bed. Sleep didn't come right away but eventually I drifted off.

With just a quick coffee, breakfast was postponed till I got back, hopefully with my wolf. Making a beeline for the spot that the wolf had disappeared into the bush I immediately found a good blood trail. He had bedded down about 50 yards inside the bush line and from the amount of blood there he couldn't have gone much further. Another 100 yards and I found another bed. This one however had a big wolf lying in it! Right on!

I had hit him just back of the chest on his left side and the bullet had exited at his second rib. Missed the heart but obviously it had done enough damage to put him down. I was so excited! Never had I even imagined having the chance to shoot a wolf, but after all my dealings with them it felt good to come out on the winning end of this deal. Boy he was a beauty. Real big and nicely furred! Flipping the partially frozen animal up onto my shoulders I fought my way to the lake shore and back to camp.

With a good fire going he should be thawed out by the time I returned from Pody Lake. As I was eating my "delicious" breakfast I realized that it was ten days till the plane was coming to get me. Funny, but now I was really looking forward to getting to town and seeing some people again. Mostly I think it was the chance for some real food that excited me. I would have to rush to make arrangements for a snowmobile when I got out also. Hopefully the bank would lend me some money till the fur sale was over. That would sure make the trip to Ahmabel and Pody lakes a lot easier. And the trails could be extended to East Ahmabel and to Fraser Lake.

With my pack loaded I strapped on my shoes and headed south west on the trail to Pody Lake. Coming up to the second trap I could see a marten hanging in the trap but something was wrong. Suddenly a squirrel jumped from the hanging marten to the tree and another squirrel landed back on the marten. By the time I reached the set the squirrels had each made a couple trips to the marten and back. Not quite sure what they had been up to I soon figured it out. They had been grabbing mouthfuls of fur off the marten; I could only imagine they were using it to line their nest or something. It was kind of funny other than the ruined fur, to watch them jump and almost franticly tear out the fur. The little critters were tag teaming him. Like they were paying this marten back for all their squirrel cousins it had ever killed.

All I knew was that my 30 dollar marten was now almost worthless. Those squirrels were sure lucky I was too lazy to carry my gun with me. By the time I reached Pody Lake I had another marten and a squirrel in my pack. With no beaver sets out here anymore I knew that my pack was not going to get to heavy today. Moving south along the lake I almost walked right past my fox set. If it wasn't for the fox jumping around I may have done just that. He had gotten caught around the middle so I guessed that I needed to make my snares a little bit smaller.

Holding him down with my axe I grabbed it by the throat and put my knee right on its heart. I could feel it beating under my knee so I applied all of my weight and in a minute the animal was dead. He was a gorgeous heavy furred red and I noticed his legs had more brown on them than normal. Like he was trying to be a cross fox but couldn't quite get there. Just to be clear a cross fox is not a cross between a silver and a red. It gets it's named from the brown stripe that runs from one front leg across the shoulders and down the other side. With the dark line that runs down the length of its back it forms a perfect cross. They really are a beautiful pelt and I wished that this one had the goods but it was not to be. The cross fox pelts were worth a lot more money.

I continued on and just before Little Pody I picked up another marten. Maybe this taking an extra day between trips is a good idea. Seems to be more fur today after the slow spell I had been having. On little Pody I came across the tracks of four wolves following my trail along the shoreline, but when I turned north up the trail they just continued down the lake. A few hundred yards in the bush I crossed the tracks of a single big wolf paralleling the lake shore. I had seen this several times before and I wondered to myself again if this animal was trying to push any prey between him and the lake out to his buddies. If that is what they were doing it would sure be a good hunting tactic. Like deer hunters bushing bush.

A short distance further Lobo charged ahead and with an explosion of wings a Ruffed grouse flew up and landed in a tree about 15 feet off the ground. Cursing myself for not bringing the gun today I look longingly at the bird sitting there. But his attention was on the dog so an idea came to mind. Moving back a ways I cut down a tall thin tree and trimmed all the branches off it. Now with the 15 foot pole in my hands I moved cautiously toward the bird. With the birds attention still on Lobo and the pole straight up in the air I lined it up and with an awkward swing nailed the bird right off its perch.

Knowing that it would probably only be stunned I rushed to where it had landed but no worries, Lobo had the grouse firmly held between his jaws. Oh boy, a good supper tonight! I thought it funny though that the bird had been so engrossed in the dog that it totally ignored me. I had an idea that if I made a small snare with the rabbit snare wire that I had brought (and obviously had no other use for), and attached it to a long pole, I could probably, by moving very slow, slip the snare right over a grouses head and snag them like that. I would try it if I ever saw another one that low to the ground. And I have caught many grouse like that since that day.

Back at camp I went down for water and there it was! A small pike on my fishing line! What a day! Fins and feathers again baby! Oh man supper was going to be a treat tonight. To top it off I made a cup of coffee to have with my supper. Strange that something as simple as a coffee with a good meal can become such a special thing all of a sudden. Just the thought of not having to eat oatmeal for even one meal was almost too much to ask for. God I hated that stuff.

With my belly full of the best meal I had eaten in a long time, my fur all hung up to thaw and a final cup of tea, I listened to some music, made some notes and let sleep take over.

(December 14)

Morning comes with the realization that I am down to about one day of flour left. That means there was going to be a week of eating nothing but oatmeal and anything that I was able to catch. Needing to keep the little bait I had for trapping I started giving Lobo some dry dog food. Pouring out a pile for him I looked at it and thought again, "What the heck". I picked one chunk up and popped it into my mouth. Hmmm... not that bad at all! Taking a few more I got busy cooking my oatmeal and bannock.

More important than the food was the fact that I was down to a half of a small jar of coffee now. That did not go over to well. I made it a little weaker to try and prolong the inevitable but I knew it was not going to last till the plane came. Washing down the bannock and oatmeal with the coffee, I packed for my day's journey while finishing my second cup.

Chain Lakes was my destination for today. As an afterthought I threw a handful of dog food into my coat pocket and got under way. With no beaver traps left set on this trail I knew I would have to start making my bait pieces really small. Crossing Hiawatha Lake I was happy to see a nice mink hanging in the first set. I moved along checking trap after trap. A Flying squirrel here and a Red squirrel there was all the action for miles. Finally I had a marten at Lake 7 but it has been half eaten by a fox. The thing would have had to stand on its hind legs to reach the hanging marten but he had managed somehow. I guess they were getting as hungry as I was.

Popping a few bites of dog food into my mouth every once in awhile I covered the miles and arrived back at the camp with nothing but a mink and a squirrel for the fur bag. Not the best day on the trap line. But I guess they all couldn't be winners.

Supper was what it was and I forced it down. At least I was not as hungry as usual since I had eaten the whole pocket of dog food. I tried to enjoy the last of the bannock knowing that from now on it was oatmeal as the staple. Oh and dog food also. Maybe I would come across a grouse or two on the trip to Ahmabel in the morning.

Darkness arrived and I sat inside pondering my situation. It is only 23 miles to the train tracks according to the game warden. My trip tomorrow would be more than half that distance. I could make it easily in two days. "No Dave, just wait for the plane" I told myself. But the thought kept nagging in the back of my mind. Sipping on my tea I wondered what Bill and Don were doing back in town. Probably eating hamburgers and drinking a beer or two. Enough of that so I turned on the radio let the music lull me to sleep. Tomorrow, like always would be another long day. About a thirteen mile return trip. But at least I didn't have to sleep in the other cabin again.

(December 15)

With the arrival of morning I found that I didn't really want to leave my bed and only the thought of a hot coffee dragged me from under the covers. With my standard oatmeal for breakfast I delayed the inevitable and for the first time I was really not looking forward to the days travel plans, and knowing that there probably wouldn't be a lot of fur in the traps made the thought of the walk a lot less exciting.

With my pack loaded and my shoes strapped on I headed north down the lake shore. Once again I munched on the dog food that Lobo had so graciously lent me. All that I was hoping for was a beaver in the one set that I had left on this trail. With a marten caught just before the Little Fraser River my spirits were buoyed a little and being such an incredibly gorgeous day it was hard to stay in a sour mood for long. My Chickadee buddies flitted along beside me for awhile and they never failed to bring a smile to my face. With a squirrel in the set just past Otter Lake I was again hopeful that there would be a beaver to eat in my snare set.

Chopping the ice away I hopefully lifted the snare pole and new right away that I had better enjoy the dog food on the way home. There was no beaver in this set. The snares were sprung however and the bait gone. Nailing some fresh bait on the dry pole and lowering it back into the water I moved on to check the otter set. The trap was sprung and what do you know. A mink had gone for the fake fish lure that I had made and I was lucky enough to have the large jaws catch him across the waist. Cool! Twice checked and I had caught an otter and a mink in my new set.

Turning back now it was going to be a long 7 mile walk back to camp. Munching on the dog food as I traveled I was just getting onto Hiawatha Lake when darkness fell. But not to worry as my trail was packed and easy to follow. Once I was back at the cabin I did my evening chores, cooked up a small batch of oatmeal and settled in to skin what I could. Which was nothing since the mink was still too wet and the marten was still frozen.

So with nothing to do and not being able to drink any coffee I sat and debated with myself about leaving early and walking out of the bush. The more I thought about it the better of an idea it seemed to me. But it was not something to try on a whim. I needed to do some planning if this was going to happen. I would still have preferred to wait for the plane. Letting the radio finally lull me to sleep again I enjoyed dreams of restaurant meals with a pretty waitress serving me my burgers and fries.

(December 16)

Today was another day to spend in camp. Sleeping in I wanted to get this day over with so I tried to make it as short as possible. What better way than to sleep late. But eventually I had to get up and eat a little. Coffee was going to be the highlight of my day I was figuring, and six hours later when I had wore myself out cutting, carrying and sawing up a ton of firewood I had to agree that Ya, the coffee had been good.

Boy it was amazing how little energy I had compared to when I had first arrived here those 7 weeks ago. The lack of quality food was taking its toll on me I was guessing, but just a few more days and I could have a feast. Not even wanting to look at a bowl of oatmeal I just ate a bunch of the dry dog food for supper and had some hot tea. The warmth of it gave me a little bit of energy so I skinned my catch from the day before and with them both stretched I crawled back into bed to rest up for the next day's trip.

Pody Lake was the destination and again I hoped for a better catch than I had been getting. Not even bothering with the radio I just closed my eyes and went to sleep.

(December 17)

Staring at the bowl of oatmeal it took all I had to stuff it down my throat. I swore to god that after this I would never eat another bite of that horrible food. But knowing I needed the energy I finished it all, and with my pack loaded I made my way out of camp and strapped on my snowshoes. My coat pockets were full of dog food (at least that had some taste to it) and as I set off toward Pody Lake I looked back and noticed that Lobo was not with me.

"Fine", I thought to myself. He can stay at camp today. He must have been as tired as I was so I would let him rest. Passing my marten traps with each one either not sprung, needing fresh bait or holding a squirrel, I was getting more and more depressed with the lack of fur production. Past wolf snares, more marten sets and the occasional mink set I could not understand where the animals had gone. Not even any wolf tracks!

Arriving at Pody Lake I turned south when suddenly I heard a wolf howl from behind me. Listening carefully and trying to pinpoint where the sound was coming from I suddenly had a chill. That was not a wolf howl. I recognized that voice! That was Lobo and there could only be one reason for him to be howling from the area that the sound was coming from.

Turning I started on a full scale run down the snowshoe trail that I had just travelled over. I just knew that he was caught in one of my wolf snares. Hopefully I would get there before he strangled himself. Tripping a couple of times I finally rounded a corner in the trail and there he was. Sitting there! He had got the snare caught around his neck and then just sat down and called for me.

Boy the relief was unreal. That was one smart dog there. Removing him from the snare, I reset it and since I was almost back at the camp I decided to return and continue this trip tomorrow. Once I was close to camp I cut down a tree for firewood and dragged it back with me. The rest of the day I spent cutting fuel for my wood stove, checking my fish lines and like usual I caught nothing. Dog food and oatmeal for supper tonight! With nothing to skin after supper I just relaxed and called it an early night.

Maybe tomorrow would bring better luck. All I could do was hope. At least it could not get worse. Just thinking of the train tracks only 20 some miles to the south made me consider walking there and hopping a train into Hornepayne. I could do it in two days easy! "But no Dave, Just get that idea out of your head and wait for your taxi". But it was still there hounding me as I fell asleep

(December 18)

Again the breakfast was just shoveled in because I knew I needed something in my belly. With my pack still loaded from the day before I moved down the trail making sure Lobo was right with me this time. To my surprise I found a nice marten in the second trap that I passed. That was a bonus and hopefully a sign of better things to come for today. But that was just a dream and as I hit Pody with not even another trap sprung, I followed the trail to my fox set.

Here I finally came across some wolf tracks and they had gone to the bait and taken it all. Now this set was useless also with no bait to replace it. So I just added some scent to the tree and hoped that it might entice a fox to investigate. On I travelled with a squirrel here and there but no marten at all. I was so tempted to reset the beaver house as I passed it but thought that even if I did the meat would not help me much since I wouldn't be back here till the day before the plane arrived.

Along the trail past Little Pody I found some grouse tracks in the snow and decided to follow them and see if I might get an opportunity to snag him. But after a 20 minute tracking job the trail ended with the marks of its wings in the snow where it had taken flight. Oh my mouth had watered as I followed that bird. But for now I just popped a few dog food pellets into my mouth and continued on my way.

Back in camp with one marten and a couple squirrels, I hung them and made myself a cup of tea. But still I couldn't get the train tracks out of my head. I stared at the map, which was cut off halfway to the tracks and I tried to visualize where the camp might be that the game warden had said was the start of the trail to the tracks. I was sure wishing that I had the whole map with me. "Never mind Dave. Just hold on, the plane is coming". I skinned the squirrels but the marten was still frozen so it would wait till morning.

Again I let the radio lull me to sleep as I tried to force the thoughts from my head. I was sleeping way too much, it was not like me and I knew it was the lack of quality food sapping my energy.

A NEW PLAN

(December 19)

Guess what! As I awoke I realized something. If I walked out of here I would save the 150 bucks that I needed for the airplane trip. And the other thing was that if I flew out how was I going to find the spot on the train tracks where the trail started. I would have no idea where to go with my snowmobile when it was time to come back. Do you remember me saying earlier about how you could rationalize anything if you wanted it bad enough, well there you go! And besides what if they forgot about me! But no they couldn't do that, my truck was parked in their driveway.

Not even repulsed by the oatmeal this morning, I made my second cup of coffee and saw that there was only enough for a couple more cups left in the jar. Another reason to leave in the morning! With the decision firmly entrenched in my brain I took off toward Chain Lakes with a new found spring in my step. Even the empty traps, the lack of grouse and the general waste of time that it seemed to be walking all those miles and not catching a thing was not enough to get me down. I was hopefully just two days away from some real food and some good coffee with cream and sugar in it.

Buy the time I had reached the Little Fraser River my pockets were empty of my travelling snacks and I was still furless for the day. As I travelled I tried to make plans for the trip tomorrow and how I would go about finding this fabled trail that would lead me to the tracks and beyond to food. My last few traps before getting to

Hiawatha Lake were empty as well. The trip along the lake went by quickly with my mind occupied on the details of the next day's travels. The other bonus of saving the airfare would be that I would have that much more money to purchase a snowmobile with.

In camp for the evening I gave Lobo a large pile of dog food and kept a bunch out for myself also. I was wondering if there would be any food left in the cabins along Nagagami Lake. Maybe, as long as they were not locked and I would replace anything that I took of course.

Finally back at camp I set about packing for my trip. Realizing right off that there was no way I was going to be taking all my fur out of here I decided that it would just be the squirrels and the weasels that would come on this trip. The Hudson Bay store in Hornepayne, like most Hudson Bay stores of that time did buy furs but of course they didn't pay what I would get at the sale. I mean they had to make a profit too, so they were only getting my squirrels so I would have some quick spending money. And by that I meant restaurant spending money! Slipping them into a bag it totaled 47 squirrels and 6 weasels, and into my pack with the axe, a good sized bag of dog food and anything else that I thought I might need. With the pack only weighing about 25 pounds I figured that I would make real good time tomorrow.

With those plans all set in my mind and the pack loaded I finished a hot tea and hit the sack. Tomorrow would for sure be a long day.

(December 20)

D-Day! It was time to leave. My plan was to follow the western shore of Nagagami Lake until I found a lodge and then look for this fabled trail to civilization. With only about half of Nagagami Lake actually on my map I was really just taking a guess. If I didn't find the trail by the time I reached the bottom of the lake I was prepared to hit the bush and compass straight south till I reached the train tracks.

And believe me, I had no illusions about getting there in one day and was fully prepared to spend a night huddled around an open fire if I had to. But hopefully I would find a lodge to stay in for the night. And oh boy would it be nice if they had left some food from the fall season.

Strapping on my long shoes I hoisted my pack and turned for one last look at my home for the last two months. A twinge of regret that I was leaving was quickly smothered by a longing for food, and then I took my first step on a long journey south. Lobo seemed to know something was different today too! He had his tail wagging and seemed more energetic somehow. Maybe it was just my imagination I thought as we walked out onto Hiawatha Lake for the last time until after the New Year.

Without another look back I followed my packed trail across the lake to my turn off point. From here on I knew it was going to be a challenge. If my directions were correct I had about 22 miles of unbroken trail to travel down over the next two days. That is not that bad of a walk on a broken trail but in this kind of snow conditions and in my physical state I knew it would test my endurance like no other trip I had been on.

From the point that I left my trail we travelled another mile and were on the ice of Nagagami Lake. Moving south down the west shoreline we went no more than a mile or so when I saw a cluster of beautiful log cabins high on an embankment overlooking the expanse of this huge lake. They looked like fairly new buildings but I was not venturing across the lake to inspect them any closer. I knew for sure that this could not be the camp that I was looking for. Staying about a quarter mile from shore for several reasons, I stayed out of the buildup of soft snow where the wind has not been able to blow it into a hard pack plus from out here I could see a lot further while looking for the cabins that may be the trail head.

Rounding the point after a few miles I was awed by the size of this lake. To my right the shore broke away to the west and then curved back in to the north. That was the bay where Pody Creek emptied into the lake and there were several islands in the bay that I wiggled my way through as I watched for buildings. I spied another group of cabins a few miles further along but this spot was still on my map so I knew that these were not the ones that I was looking for either. This second group was actually one huge building with some out buildings around it. I passed fairly close to it and then cut across a big bay to hit a long skinny point that jutted out into the lake at a northeast angle.

From this point on I was mapless! I had hit the cutoff spot and now would go by guesswork. With the deep snow I was figuring that I must have been doing about 2 miles an hour. Having to stop every once in awhile to rest from the heavy trail breaking was really slowing me down. In several places I could feel a buildup of slush under the snows surface but in each case I was able to stay on top of it and not have to worry about my shoes icing up. But no need to over exert myself, I did have a long way to go and I knew I would not get there today. Rounding the point I followed the shore west, and soon came upon another group of cabins. If the other camps had looked quite new then these were their grandfathers. Very well built and in great shape but they did look like they had been here for a long time.

In front of the main cabin, stood three of the biggest trees that I had ever seen, they were White spruce and two of them had to be five feet across at the base. They were even bigger that the huge White pine trees that grew north of the Severn River, back where I trapped just north of Orillia.

But the good news was that I now had a place to spend the night. I just hoped that the door was open. I tried it and sure enough it was unlocked. As I said before, most cabins in the "north country" were not locked in case someone got stranded. And besides, locks only keep honest people out and if someone wanted to steal your stuff, a locked door only meant that you would have a broken door to fix on top of things. Inside I prayed, and sure enough my prayers were answered. I found some coffee but the only food was a pound of lard in a sealed pail. I was not that hungry yet! Taking the large cooking pot I brought some snow inside to melt for water and built a fire in the wood stove.

With the snow melting I decided to strap my shoes back on and take a look around for the trail. It didn't take me long to figure out that it could not be this camp that I was looking for. The trail was supposed to head south and from here south was across the lake. But just in case I did a walk around the camp. There was a trail heading off to the north but it only went in about a quarter mile to an opening where they had been cutting their fire wood. Finishing my circle I was satisfied that this was not the spot. But it was sure a nice spot to spend the night. Even an actual bed, with blankets and all! And to top it off there were pillows!

With an hour of daylight left I just relaxed, melted snow, and drank coffee like I had just invented it. Ya, it sure beat sleeping in front of an open fire all night eating dog food and snow. This was like heaven! Funny though, all the walking I had done in the past weeks and this one day had tested my legs more than any other day. The miles of breaking trail was a test for sure and it felt good to kick back and relax while sipping on a coffee. Even if my meal was just dry dog food. I felt like a king! And tomorrow I would reach the outside world again. Off to the south I heard a sound that slowly grew louder and louder. It was moving from east to west and seemed like it was very close. The train tracks could not be that far away if I could hear it that clearly.

Soon the sky was dark and with nothing else to do I decide to hit the sack. It was only about 7 o'clock but I guess I needed the sleep because I never moved till the morning sun was just lightening the eastern sky.

BACK TO CIVILIZATION AND REAL FOOD

(December 21)

By the time the sun completely cleared the horizon I was out the door, into the cold clear air and hooking up my snowshoes. I had probably been asleep for near 12 hours so I was well rested and ready to go. Having had two hot cups of java and a few handfuls of munchies I turned southeast and make tracks for the point directly across the bay from this camp. Aiming to cross between the shore and a tiny island I covered the mile in 20 minutes and moved down the shore.

Only a mile past the island I rounded a point and there lay another cluster of cabins. This had to be the spot that I had been looking for. Climbing the steep trail from the lake level to the top of the embankment that the lodge was built on, I tried to decide where to look first for the trail. Behind the main cabin there was a trail heading into the bush, but following it I found nothing but a huge pile of empty 45 gallon fuel drums. Backtracking to the lake shore, I then followed a trail along the edge of the shore, past the last cabin, past the boats, all pulled up on shore and flipped over, past the bulldozer parked in an opening beside the trail and on, until I was again surrounded by the forest. Now this however was a real trail. Twelve feet wide, and for the most part straight as an arrow! I could see several hundred yards in front of me and then the trail would take a turn to run on for another distance before turning to miss a hill or some other obstacle. It was a mystery to me why there would be a need for a trail this wide, but was to later find out that it was used to haul 45 gallon drums of fuel in for the entire fishing season.

However many miles and a couple of hours later, I was starting to wonder if I was even on the right trail. From the sound of the train the night before I didn't think it would be this far. My compass told me I "could" be going in the right direction, but I wasn't heading straight south, it was more south west and I began to think that someone out here just made really nice trapping trails.

Continuing on I passed swamp after swamp until the bush parted and there it was. Twin rails of steel for as far as the eye could see in both directions. Here I had no problem knowing which way to turn! Left was the way to town, and I never even let a minute go by as I unstrapped my snowshoes and attached them to my packsack. Walking between the rails was an adventure, after weeks of snowshoeing, to suddenly have to try and walk on those ties. They were not at a proper distance for my steps, and I have never felt more spazzy than the first few hundred yards of that trip.

Just east of where I connected with the tracks was a sign that read "20". Not sure but I guessed that it was a mileage marker. Really, I was still twenty miles from Hornepayne? I sure hopped I was not going to have to walk the entire distance into town. The minutes turned into an hour and the steps, awkward as they were, turned into miles. And by now I was sure the signs were counting down the miles from town. It was kind of nice to walk without my snowshoes on and have something solid to step on but the odd spacing of the ties really could drive you nuts. A big step then a little one, then two little ones and a big one! There was just no rhythm to it and by the time I passed the 16 mile marker I was praying for a train to come by.

A short distance further I crossed over a large river that was signed as the Obuckimaga River. It was flowing north, so I guessed that it flowed into the south end of Nagagami Lake. I figured that maybe

I could use it to access my trap line in the fall and save on the plane trips. A few minutes later I heard the sound of an approaching train, and the good news was that it was coming from the right direction. I could see the headlights from a long ways off, and it took at least ten minutes to get to where I was. I pulled Lobo off the tracks, and waved my arms over my head and instantly heard the engines rev down. Yes, they were going to stop!

But as it pulled up beside me the train just blew right by. However it seemed to still be slowing down and as the caboose got closer I could see someone sticking their head out of a window on the last car. As the train rolled past someone yelled that they would be stopped shortly, and to hurry and follow if I needed a ride. I didn't really "need" a ride but I sure as heck wanted one. Running down the tracks for a hundred yards the train finally stopped, and Lobo and I climbed aboard.

The brakeman radioed to the engineer to get under way as they offered me a seat and a coffee. After 8 weeks of not a word to another person, I just sort of sat there drinking my coffee as they stared at me. I think that after that long in the bush without a mirror or a shower, I must have been a sight. Especially living in a dirt floor cabin! It took just a few minutes till one of them asked me a question. When I answered it, the flood gates were opened. It was like they had been trying to decide whether I could talk or not.

"Where did I come from", and "What, how long have you been in there", along with a million other questions. It was like an assault on my brain. I was actually unnerved and I think they saw it and backed off a little. This must be what it would be like to get questioned by the police. After a bit my eyes closed from the heat in the caboose and I dozed off for awhile. The sound of the train slowing woke me, and the guys told me that we were on a siding waiting for another train to pass us. Soon enough a passenger train zoomed past heading west at a good clip.

At the beginning of my story I had mentioned the book Traplines North. Well in the book the author Stephen W. Meader tells of arriving at the Nakina train station on the local passenger train. He could have come down this very set of tracks that I was now travelling on. It had to be this set of tracks or the one coming from Cochrane. Those were the only two options. Nakina was only about a hundred miles west and north of here. That was so cool thinking that the book that started my interest in trapping may have had a connection to where I was right now.

Once the passenger train was past we started under way again and soon we were entering the Hornepayne train yard. They mentioned that I would have about a mile walk from where we stopped to get into town. "No problem" I replied. "Better than the 16 miles it would have been if you hadn't picked me up".

Once we came to a stop Lobo and I got out, said thanks and got directions through the yard. It was a huge sprawling maze of train tracks and trains all leading to the station at the center of town. Not more than a block from the station was the Hudson Bay Company store. And to my pleasure right across the road from that store was a wonderful looking restaurant. With Lobo tied up to his beaver pulling rope, I dropped my pack at the door, removed the bag of furs, and tied him to the pack. Inside I asked for the manager, and then asked him if he was buying furs. Thankfully he said yes and I brought out my furs explaining that all I had been able to carry out of the bush were these little guys. Accepting an offer of a dollar each, I pocketed the $53.00 and he asked that when I returned with the rest of my fur if I would give him a chance to make an offer for it. I told him sure, and made my way straight across the road.

Oh the smell of that place as I walked through the door. Maybe the waitress and patrons said the same about me, but I didn't care. There was real food just a few minutes away. The waitress brought me a menu and I waived it away asking for a coffee, a can of coke and a bacon cheese burger, with a side order of fries. Oh and while you are at it bring me another burger as well. I must have been a sight, since everyone seemed to be staring at me, so I went into the bathroom and checked the mirror. Oh my god, I was out in public like this! Giving my face a good scrub in the sink, I finally returned and my food was on the table waiting for me.

Oh man, I didn't know where to start so I lifted the can of coke and let the bubbles slide down my throat! Are you getting the picture? I was enjoying this to the max. Savoring every bite, I had myself a third cup of coffee and then paid, and stepped outside with my second burger. Dropping it on the ground for Lobo I sat beside him and tried to figure out what was next. It was too late to try thumbing a ride tonight so I needed a place to stay. Not wanting to spend the rest of my money on a hotel room, I remembered that there was a Y.M.C.A. in town.

Making my way there I got a room for just a few bucks, and had a shower that must have washed five pounds of dirt off of me. Suddenly I felt totally beat, and as I crawled into bed I could hear the music from the bar down the street. It slowly drowned out as my mind shut down.

(December 22)

Waking in the morning with a hunger on, I was back at the restaurant at seven and had my first eggs in a long time. With a few coffees under my belt, I walked down to the highway and stuck out my thumb. An hour later and only the third vehicle to go by was my ticket to Highway # 11. This fellow was heading west on Hwy# 11, and my truck was to the east, so I thanked him and started walking. A short time later I was again dropped off, but this time right at the air services where my truck was waiting for me.

Knocking on the office door I was greeted with surprise that I had walked out. "Sorry", they said, "We were planning on putting a charger on your battery for you, so it would be ready for you when you got out of the plane, but I guess we can just boost it if it won't start". And it wouldn't! At least they hadn't forgotten about me. So with their help I was again mobile and heading home a short half hour later. The next two hours went by quickly as I drove south, passing Hornepayne and then arriving in White River, the town made famous as the birth place of Winnie-the-Pooh, and as the coldest spot in Canada. 72 degrees below zero! Now that, my friends, is cold!

Pulling into the Green Gables Hotel parking lot the first vehicle I saw was Bills' truck. "Must be in having an afternoon beer", I thought to myself. Opening the door I could see Bill at a table and Dennie behind the bar. Both came up and with a slap on the back said, "Holy crap, we never expected to see you again". That's weird I thought to myself, "It's only the bush, what could go wrong".

EPILOGUE

For the next two weeks I worked at the bar and made some money to pay for my return trip into the bush. I needed a snowmobile, and with Dennies connections, was able to purchase (with the banks help), a new Arctic Cat snow machine. The first week of January saw me on the road north again, with a big load of supplies to haul in with my machine. Breaking trail all the way from Hornepayne along the tracks turned out to be a challenge as well. I had never even sat on a snowmobile before this so you can imagine the fun I was having. Only making it half way down the tracks the first day, I ended up sleeping in an abandoned cabin on the side of the tracks. The second night found me again at the same camp I had stayed at on the walk out. The third night found me at my camp, with my snowmobile stuck in the slush of Nagagami Lake, six miles back.

The next morning I walked back, and learned my first lesson of snowmobile travel in the north. Any lake you cross, you need to snowshoe a trail first, and always travel the same trail afterwards. That way it is good for the season. After a few hours of chopping and lifting, I was able to continue on my way along my now packed trail.

Between crashing into trees, and getting stuck in the slush about a thousand times, I learned a lot about where a snowmobile can and can't go over the following months. Two weeks later I brought my fur all out and kept my promise to the Hudson Bay store manager.

He didn't offer me what I wanted, so my catch got shipped off to North Bay and the O.T.A. fur sale.

The rest of the winter passed by with me cutting trails by hand since I couldn't afford a chainsaw until my fur check came in, and by that time the winter was over. After that first trip along the tracks, the snowmobiling got easier, because I just left the machine at the trail head and took the train back and forth each time. Later that winter, I had the privilege of meeting another very influential person in my life at that time, by the name of Joe Kuhl , pronounced "Cool", and he truly was. I will tell you some stories about Joe if I ever write another book, cause he was a heck of a guy!

Sooner than I wanted, my first year trapping in the northern wilderness ground to a halt. With my catch ending up being 43 beaver, 61 marten, 11 mink, 4 otter, 3 wolves, 3 fox, 67 squirrels and 9 weasels it was not the greatest catch in the world but for a greenhorn kid from southern Ontario, I was more than happy with it. That winter confirmed that I had truly chosen the right course for my life. It was honestly a blast! And now, finally, I can at least look at, but still not eat oatmeal!

Come spring time I was able to get a job that paid well, and fit perfectly into my trapping schedule. I started fighting forest fires for the Ontario Natural Resources department. This was an amazing job for a young guy, flying into hot spots in a helicopter putting out a fire and moving on to the next one. I figured it out one time that between firefighting and trapping I would spend 250 - 275 nights a year in the bush. We travelled to places all over the province and at times to other parts of the country when there were "fire flaps" picking up and the local fire teams were over worked. The fire season started in May, right after trapping was done and it ended in September, just before trapping started. It couldn't have been any better if I had of planned it out myself.

Oh and I finally, later that winter, found out why God had invented slush and Tag alders. The tags were used to mark trails across the slush and the slush was there so the tags would have a purpose. The perfect symbiotic relationship... Dave Vander Meer

Glossary of Important Locations

Hiawatha Cabin	49 degrees 30' 24" N	by	85 degrees 00' 49.3" W
Ahmabel Camp	49 degrees 35' 35.5" N	by	84 degrees 55' 16" W
Moose In River	49 degrees 30' 53" N	by	84 degrees 59' 33" W
Sharptail Migration	49 degrees 35' 49" N	by	84 degrees 55' 01" W
Wolf Pack in Dark	49 degrees 29' 53" N	by	84 degrees 59' 50" W
Fall through the Ice	49 degrees 31' 47" N	by	85 degrees 00' 40" W
Little Pody Trail	49 degrees 29' 14" N	by	85 degrees 03' 07" W
Fraser Lake	49 degrees 32' 48" N	by	84 degrees 55' 14" W
East Ahmabel Lake	49 degrees 34' 40" N	by	84 degrees 52' 14" W
Scuckasu Lake	49 degrees 37' 00" N	by	84 degrees 55' 46" W
Joe Kuhls Camp	49 degrees 24' 07" N	by	85 degrees 03'14" W
Trail Head on CNR	49 degrees 21' 28" N	by	85 degrees 07' 15" W
Overnight Camp on Trip out	49 degrees 25' 06" N	by	85 degrees 04' 54" W
Chain Lake # 3	49 degrees 29' 52" N	by	84 degrees 58' 57" W
Chain Lake Trail	49 degrees 29.5' 74" N	by	84 degrees 59' 50" W
Little Fraser River Trail	49 degrees 32' 15" N	by	85 degrees 00' 31.5" W
Chasing Wolf in Trap	49 degrees 31' 10" N	by	85 degrees 00' 04" W

Check out these coordinates on a map site, like Google Earth. Notice that my hope that the lumber companies would never get that far in did not hold up. Huge tracts of that line have since been cleared off. Although in the long run it would definitely be better for the beaver population it is still sad to see that another wilderness area that will never be the same.

ABOUT THE AUTHOR

The author at the age of 13 began trapping the farmland just an hour north of Toronto, Ontario where he resided. At 16 he took the first trapper instructor course ever held. At 20 years of age he became the youngest licensed trapping instructor in Ontario and has since that time has trapped several trap lines in the remote northern wilderness.

Now living in Manitoba where he operates Sleeping Giants Outfitters, a Whitetail deer and Black bear hunting operation in the Duck Mountains of central Manitoba. He continues to trap on a registered trapline near his home north of Grandview Manitoba, Canada.